THE LITTLE

BARBECUE

THE LITTLE GUIDES

BARBECUE

FOG CITY PRESS

Published by Fog City Press
814 Montgomery Street
San Francisco, CA 94133 USA

Copyright © 2004 Weldon Owen Pty Ltd
Reprinted in 2004, 2005

Chief Executive Officer: John Owen
President: Terry Newell
Publisher: Lynn Humphries
Managing Editor: Janine Flew
Design Manager: Helen Perks
Editorial Coordinator: Jennifer Losco
Production Manager: Caroline Webber
Production Coordinator: Monique Layt
Sales Manager: Emily Jahn
Vice President International Sales: Stuart Laurence

Project Editor: Janine Flew
Designer: Helen Perks

A catalog record for this book is available from
the Library of Congress, Washington, D.C.

ISBN 1 877019 91 7

Color reproduction by Colourscan Co Pte Ltd
Printed by SNP Leefung Printers Ltd
Printed in China

A Weldon Owen Production

CONTENTS

PART TWO
RECIPES

Introduction

A rchaeological evidence indicates that humans have been grilling food over open fires for at least 125,000 years. Barbecuing was humankind's first cooking method, and it's still one of the most popular. Most cultures have their own version of the grill. The Brazilian *churrasco*, Japanese *hibachi*, Greek *souvlaki*, Indian *tandoor* and Middle Eastern *kofta* all belong to this ancient tradition. People around the world seem to agree on at least one point: that barbecuing delivers the most flavor, and the most fun.

Barbecuing is perhaps the most evocative of cooking styles, reminiscent of relaxed summer days spent outdoors with family and friends. It's an easy and convivial way to cook for a crowd. Guests tend to gather around the barbecue to watch the action, contributing to the process themselves and also involving the cook much more than if he or she were in the kitchen, as for a regular meal.

In recent years, barbecuing has surged in popularity, resulting in a vast array of fancy grills and an even wider range of foods to cook on them. Today's barbecue may feature spice-rubbed pork loin, a side of salmon slowly smoking over cedar chips, shrimp skewers or a platter of char-grilled vegetables. Yet the traditional favorites such as burgers and chicken wings still retain their homey appeal.

While the barbecue aficionado may opt for a top-range grill with a battery of sophisticated attachments, barbecuing at its most basic simply requires a grill, fuel and something to cook. And whether you opt for a simple or complex set-up, the rewards of barbecuing remain the same: the smoky flavor and delicious charring that no other cooking method can match.

Barbecuing offers something for everyone. It lends itself to all types of meat, poultry and seafood, as well as vegetables, tofu and some cheeses. Even better, it's no longer limited only to those with plenty of yard space. The invention of compact electric indoor grills has brought the barbecue indoors, a boon to apartment dwellers and others with limited outdoor access.

This compact guide is divided into two parts. Part One instructs you in the basics of choosing, fueling and caring for your grill. Also included is information on marinating food, food safety, cooking times and barbecue accessories, as well as tips for success. Part Two provides more than 110 recipes from all over the world, for both outdoor and indoor grills. Finally, a handy glossary gives hints on choosing, storing and using ingredients called for in the recipes.

So, whether you want a simple family meal or a multi-course feast for a special occasion, choose a recipe from this book, fire up the grill and enjoy all the fun and flavor of barbecue.

PART ONE

THE BASICS

This section covers the various types of grills available, how to use and care for them, and the different ways you can cook using them. Charts of grilling times are also given, along with tips on food preparation and food safety.

Grilling and Barbecuing

Although the terms grilling and barbecuing are often used interchangeably, and both refer to methods of live-fire cooking, there are differences. Grilling is a direct-heat method in which foods are quickly cooked over live flames or hot coals. Home grills operate at temperatures in excess of 500°F (240°C); some restaurant grills reach temperatures of up to 1000°F (540°C). Such high heat chars the outside of the food, sealing in juices and producing a smoky, crisp crust.

Grilling best suits small or thin, tender cuts of meat, such as steaks, sausages, chops, burgers, kabobs or chicken breasts or pieces. Small whole fish or shellfish are also suitable, as are vegetables and even breads.

Barbecuing, on the other hand, is a long, slow, indirect-heat method of cooking. "Indirect heat" means that the food is cooked some way away from the fire source, which is usually smoldering logs, charcoal or wood chunks. When barbecuing with a gas or charcoal grill, the flames are allowed to die down on one side or around the edges of the grill and the food is placed on the other side or in the center. This method of cooking is ideally suited to large pieces of meat, such as legs or shoulders, or whole pigs, chickens or turkeys. Barbecuing is also excellent for briskets, spareribs and other cheaper cuts of meat. These cuts are flavorsome, but have more tough connective tissue than expensive cuts; however, this breaks down during the long, slow cooking, producing meltingly tender results.

Barbecued food gets its flavor from charring and smoke. Smoke is a natural preservative; in former times, food was smoked to make it keep longer.

Outdoor Grills

Barbecuing is traditionally done outdoors, and there are many types of outdoor grills available. Some modules closely resemble the kitchen stove and make it possible to include succulent roasts, spicy curries, casseroles and seafood in your barbecue menus. Even old favorites such as steaks, chops and sausages stand a better chance of being cooked well. Mastering the art of barbecue cooking isn't hard. Choose the type of grill that suits you best, then follow the basic rules (see pages 24–25) for success.

When you buy an outdoor grill, study the manufacturer's instructions carefully—different models require specific know-how to get the best out of them.

PORTABLE GRILLS

These simply constructed grills consist of a grate holding the fuel—usually charcoal—and a grill rack positioned above the hot coals. In some models, the grill rack can be raised or lowered. Look for a sturdy model on solid legs so there's less danger of it tipping over. Air vents will make it easier to control the cooking heat and handles that don't get hot are essential if you want to move your grill for any reason before the fire cools. The best-known portable grill is the hibachi—the Japanese word for firebowl.

GAS AND ELECTRIC GRILLS

In these models, volcanic lava rock, ceramic briquets or metal bars are heated by a gas flame or electric element. The temperature can be set and adjusted easily. Gas models are quick, making them particularly good if you decide to have a barbecue at short notice.

Look for sturdy construction in a gas or electric grill and two or more heating zones. A built-in thermometer removes some of the guesswork and a tight-fitting lid allows you added versatility in cooking methods. Some models can be fitted with a rotisserie and smoking box.

WOOD-FUELED GRILLS

These are usually table-type grills custom-built in your backyard or are the type you find in recreation parks and at communal functions. When the wood has burned down to glowing coals, the grill is ready to use. The cooking surface is either a solid plate or a grill rack or a combination of both.

COVERED, KETTLE-TYPE OR TURBO GRILLS

All the types of grill previously discussed are suitable for steaks, sausages, burgers, kabobs and all small, flat cuts of meat. But to cook large cuts by the indirect heat method, a covered kettle-type grill is essential. These can be round or square. The heat is controlled by vents on the bottom as well as on the lid.

These grills produce such wonderful roasts that you'll wonder why you ever bothered with a conventional kitchen oven. They can also be used for smoking. Another advantage of covered grills is that they deflect wind and rain, allowing you to barbecue in inclement weather.

Roasting in Kettle Grills

A boon for the busy cook, kettle grills require very little preparation and the roast can be left to virtually cook by itself.

PREPARATION TIPS

• Allow the grill to heat with the lid off. The heat is too intense when first lit, so wait for the coals to turn white before you start cooking. This will take about 1 hour, so allow for it in your schedule. Rake hot coals to the sides of the grill, around a foil drip pan placed in the center of the grill for indirect cooking.

• To maximize tenderness, take small roasts from the refrigerator 15 minutes prior to cooking. For larger roasts, allow 30 minutes.

• Trim excess fat from meat to prevent spatter and flare-ups. Position meat directly over the foil pan to catch drips.

• To keep meat moist during cooking and to add flavor, brush with a baste or marinade (see page 42).

COOKING TIPS

• Roast meat with the lid on and the vent open for the calculated time, basting occasionally with pan juices or a marinade.

• Remove roast from grill. Cover and leave to rest in a warm place before carving. (Resting keeps roasts juicy.) Small roasts need about 10 minutes' resting and larger ones about 20 minutes.

Keep in mind that the internal temperature of meat and poultry will rise slightly during resting, so allow for this when calculating roasting times.

ROASTING TIMES

For small roasts—those weighing ¾ lb–1 lb (360–480 g)—allow 7–8 minutes' cooking time per 4 oz (120 g) for medium meat. Total roasting time will be about 30 minutes.

For larger roasts—1½–2 lb (720–960 g)—allow about 30 minutes per 1 lb (480 g) for medium meat. Total roasting time will be 45–60 minutes.

Fueling Your Grill

There are many different types of grill fuel available. Purists maintain that there is simply no substitute for wood; charcoal enthusiasts extol its virtues; advocates of the heat bead or briquet praise the enduring heat; gas fans love its instant response. The truth is that no one fuel is better than another. Each has advantages and each gives good results when used correctly.

GAS

Most gas grills have two or more burners with separate controls, which makes them economical —you don't have to heat the entire cooking area for just a few chops. The food is not cooked by the gas flames but by radiated heat. Some models use metal bars coated with porcelain or vitreous enamel to distribute the heat, but the more usual material is chunks of natural lava or compressed lava compounds. Meat juices and fats falling on the hot distributor create steam and smoke that fill the air with the familiar barbecue smell and impart characteristic flavor to the food. Frequent flare-ups indicate cleaning is needed.

Always scrape your grill plate thoroughly as you heat it, to remove any bits stuck on from the last time it was used. After the barbecue, allow the lava to cool then soak it overnight in a bucket of hot water and dish-washer detergent, rinse well under running water and leave it out in the sun to dry.

WOOD

Different woods give distinctly different flavors.

Alder gives a light, clean flavor suited to chicken, turkey and fresh salmon.

Apple has a clean, tangy flavor that goes with chicken, pork and game.

Cherry is sweet, with distinct cherry overtones. It suits duck and other poultry.

Grapevine prunings burn at a high heat and impart a clean flavor that suits steaks, other meats and seafood.

Hickory is a favorite and the traditional wood for American barbecues. Rich and smoky, it teams well with pork.

Maple is mild, sweet-smelling and mellow. Use it for pork, poultry and seafood.

Mesquite has a robust, smoky flavor and is popular for beef.

Oak is a European favorite. Its clean, well-balanced flavor complements seafood, poultry and meat.

More resinous woods, such as pine and eucalypts, can impart a bitter taste to the food. Never use old building materials—painted or treated wood can give off poisonous fumes.

For best results, wood must be quite dry. Firelighters should not be necessary—just some scrunched-up paper, twigs for kindling and then the larger pieces of wood. Position the fire where a breeze can flow through; the flames should flare up and quickly die down to form embers. Wait until there is a bed of glowing embers before heating the grill or hotplate and don't put the food on until all the flames have died down. If there are flames, the meat will be singed on the outside and raw in the center.

Smoking

For a lovely smoky flavor, make "logs" of your chosen wood by wrapping chips, pre-soaked in water, in foil. Place the foil "log" on the hot fuel or lava and wait for 10 minutes or so until it begins to smolder and smoke. A log made with about 4 oz (120 g) wood chips should go on smoking for a good half-hour. This method is especially effective in a covered grill. The woody stems of such herbs as rosemary, or bundles of dried or fresh herbs, can also add another dimension to the flavor. Soak then drain the herbs or stems before using them.

CHARCOAL

Charcoal is a form of charred wood; despite its name, it has nothing to do with coal, which is a carbon-based mineral. It is commercially produced by burning wood slowly without allowing complete combustion. Deprived of oxygen, the wood smolders, evaporating the water and resins in the wood but not consuming all its combustible elements. Charcoal burns more cleanly, more efficiently and at higher temperatures than wood. It is readily available and easy to store (always keep it dry).

There are three basic types: **Charwood**, also known as lump charcoal or chunk charwood charcoal, is made by burning whole logs or large chunks of wood in a kiln without oxygen. It is sold in irregularly shaped pieces and is the form preferred by professional grill chefs. **Natural briquets** are small, regularly shaped pieces of pulverized charcoal held together with natural starches. **Composition briquets** are made from burned wood, wood scraps and/or coal dust, and are bound together with paraffin or petroleum products.

Once it is glowing, charcoal gives off excellent heat. If you want to save the charcoal for future use once the food is cooked, simply pour on water to extinguish the fire and allow the coals to dry out before using them again. Grilling over charcoal imparts a delicious wood-smoky flavor to foods.

On the downside, charcoal can be hard to light—you may have to use firelighters or paraffin starter cubes. Petroleum-based starter fluids are also an option, but these must be used with care. Also, a charcoal fire may not last quite long enough to cook large pieces of meat. This problem can be easily overcome by burning heat beads along with the charcoal.

Use enough briquets so that when spread out in a single layer, they will extend slightly beyond the cooking area.

STEP 1

Lighting Charcoal

Arrange the charcoal briquets in a pyramid in the center of the lower grill rack. If they are self-lighting, ignite them with a match. If they are regular briquets, use an electric starter or chimney device or squirt them with lighter fluid and then ignite. The briquets are ready when covered with a gray ash, after 30–40 minutes for regular, 5–10 minutes for self-lighting.

Use the direct-heat method for grilling small or thin pieces of meat or poultry, or vegetables.

STEP 2

Briquets for Direct Heat

For direct-heat grilling, use long-handled tongs and spread the hot coals in a single layer across the grate. Food will cook more evenly if the coals are arranged with about 1/2 inch (1 cm) of space between each briquet.

Use the
indirect-heat
method for
grilling whole
chickens, turkeys
or fish, or large
pieces of meat.

STEP 3

Briquets for Indirect Heat

For indirect-heat grilling, arrange the hot coals around
the edge of the grill, leaving a space in the center. Set
a disposable foil drip pan in the middle so that it is
surrounded by briquets. The food is placed on the
upper grill rack over the drip pan, then the grill is
covered so that heat and smoke circulate evenly.

Hold your hand
in the center of
the grill above the
coals or pan to
test the heat.

STEP 4

Testing Heat of Coals

Check the temperature by holding your hand, palm-side
down, at about the height at which the food will cook.
If you must pull your hand away after 2 seconds, the
coals are hot; 3 seconds, medium hot; 4 seconds,
medium; 5 seconds, medium slow; 6 seconds, slow.
When grilling with indirect heat, the temperature of
the coals should be one level hotter than the desired
temperature over the drip pan.

Char-grilling

Successful char-grilling takes patience; don't be tempted to start cooking until your fire is just right. Get to know your grill—where its hottest spots are and how long it takes to reach the optimum temperature for a sizzling performance.

PREPARATION TIPS

Trim any excess fat from the meat to prevent spatter and flare-ups. Marinate meat for at least 1 hour, or overnight if possible. (Overnight marination should be done in the refrigerator.) The longer you marinate, the more intense the flavor will be. To maximize tenderness, remove meat from refrigerator 15 minutes prior to cooking. If desired, brush the meat with the remaining marinade once or twice during cooking to keep it moist and to give extra flavor.

STEPS FOR CHAR-GRILLING

Heat the grill on high. (For wood or charcoal grills, heat to glowing coals. There must be no flames.) Place the meat on the grill and allow it to brown and seal well before turning it over with tongs. The amount of time it takes to sear will depend on the size and thickness of the cut. As a general rule, when juices appear on the uncooked side of the meat, this is a good indication that it's time to turn.

Cook the other side of the meat until it is browned and sealed. It's important not to keep on turning the meat. Frequent turning doesn't seal the meat well enough to keep in the juices and it becomes dry and tough. For the same reason, don't pierce or cut the meat with a fork or knife. Cook the meat until it is done to your liking (see pages 28–29).

Rotisserie Grilling

Also known as spit-roasting, this is a good way to cook large food items, such as roasts and whole birds. A rotisserie attachment is an optional extra with most gas grills and some charcoal grills. It consists of a large, electric-powered spit that turns at a slow, constant speed above the heat source. Many foods that are cooked over indirect heat can also be cooked on a rotisserie. The timing will be similar.

When using a rotisserie, be sure to balance the food as evenly as possible on the spit. Unbalanced food will cause the motor to strain and jerk, causing uneven cooking and undue stress on the motor. However, most rotisseries come with a counterweight system that can be adjusted to compensate for the irregular shape of certain foods.

Rotisseries differ considerably according to brand and type, so become familiar with the instructions for your particular rotisserie when assembling it and cooking with it.

To grill foods on a rotisserie, first prepare a fire for indirect-heat cooking. Using strong kitchen string made of cotton or jute (never synthetic materials), truss whole birds or tie roasts into neat, compact shapes. Thread the food onto the spit, following the manufacturer's instructions. (This task is easier with two people.) Insert the spit into the rotisserie mechanism according to the manufacturer's instructions and position the food above the drip pan. Turn on the rotisserie motor and cook the food according to the recipe or until done to your liking. The food will baste itself as it turns, but if you like, you can baste it occasionally with a marinade or the pan drippings.

To check if the food is cooked, test with an instant-read thermometer, or cut into the food. See pages 30–33 for doneness tests.

Caring for Your Grill

Although grills are fairly low-maintenance items, they do require some care. Follow these basic instructions, and a good-quality grill will cook cleanly and efficiently for years.

• Before using a grill for the first time, always read the owners' manual supplied with it. Note the cleaning instructions, too.

• Before you start cooking, brush a little oil on the grill rack to prevent food from sticking and to make cleanup easier.

• After cooking, while the grill is still hot, use a long-handled wire brush to remove any bits of food stuck to the grill rack. Cover the grill and allow the residual heat to burn off the residue.

• For charcoal grills, clean out the fire bed frequently to prevent ashes accumulating. When the ash is completely cold, scoop it out and discard it in a nonflammable container.

• For gas grills, let the ceramic briquets or lava rocks cool completely, then sort through them and remove and discard bits of food that could clog the gas jets. Heavily soiled briquets or rocks will not heat efficiently;

they should be discarded and replaced with fresh ones. Do not wash rocks or briquets with detergent.

• Do not line the grill rack or fire bed with material of any kind. Grills attain very high temperatures, and foreign matter may ignite and cause a fire hazard. (Aluminum foil will not ignite, but it will impede the essential flow of air, and so should not be used.)

• Always protect your grill with a waterproof cover, or store it indoors.

23

Accessories

You don't need a lot of special equipment for barbecuing, but the following items will make the job easier and safer:

• a heavy-duty apron to protect your clothes

• long oven mitts to protect arms and hands

• long matches or tapers for safer lighting up

• long-handled tongs—one set to move hot coals and wood around, the other to turn food

• sturdy brushes for basting food during cooking (a long-handled one will protect your hands against fire)

• drip pans if you are grilling by indirect heat

• a water spray for dousing flare-ups on solid-fuel grills (but never spray water on a gas grill—with gas grills, move the food away from the flame and make a mental note to clean the lava before you use it again)

• scrapers and cleaning brushes

• skewers, to make small items of food manageable. Metal ones are best; bamboo ones must first be soaked in cold water for about 1 hour to prevent them scorching

• a spatula to lift delicate items (some have a serrated edge to get under the food)

• a hinged basket that holds fish or several chops or sausages at a time, making it easy to turn them all over together.

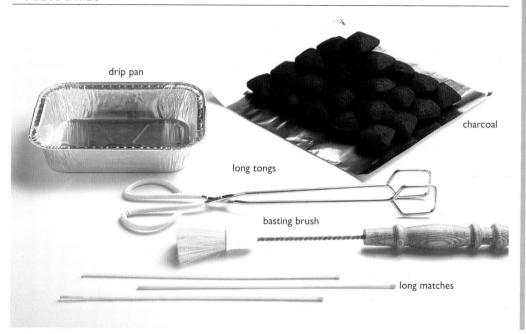

drip pan

charcoal

long tongs

basting brush

long matches

Tips for Great Grilling

STEAK

• Trim the meat of any excess external fat. Internal fat, or marbling, increases tenderness and flavor, but external fat causes flare-ups as it melts and drips into the fire. Removing fat also reduces your fat intake.

• Nick the edges, particularly of thinner steaks, to stop the meat curling during cooking.

• Don't season meat with salt before cooking; salt draws out the essential juices that keep it moist and may produce a dry, tough steak.

• Marinate the steak. This helps tenderize the less-expensive cuts and also enables you to add a variety of flavors to your meat. When possible, marinate overnight to allow flavors to develop. An hour will be sufficient if you're in a hurry. (See page 42 for further information on marinating.)

• Make sure the grill is well heated, but remember that you want heat to cook the meat, not flame. Charcoal or wood grills should be allowed to burn down to glowing coals.

• Drain the meat from the marinade; place it on the grill. Cook until well sealed, about 3 minutes on each side. For a rare steak, remove and serve. For medium meat, reduce heat to medium (if using a gas or electric grill) or move the meat to a cooler part of a charcoal or wood grill. Cook until the meat is slightly springy to the touch, a further 2–3 minutes each side (a total of 4–6 minutes each side). For well-done steak, cook for a further 4–6 minutes each side (a total of 6–9 minutes each side). To lock in the juices that keep the meat moist and tender, don't turn it too often.

• Let your steak rest in a warm place for 3–15 minutes after grilling, depending on the size of the cut, to allow the juices to redistribute throughout the meat. This ensures juiciness and full flavor. Keep in mind that the meat will keep cooking while it rests, so remove it from the grill when it is still a little off the desired degree of doneness.

SAUSAGES

• Sausages should not be pricked or they will burst and the juices will cause flare-ups. Also, they will shrivel and become dry. The secret to super, non-exploding sausages is to cook them slowly on the coolest section of the grill. Thick sausages take 15–20 minutes.

• To shorten the grilling time and to remove some of the fat, partly cook sausages by placing them in a saucepan of cold water and bringing them to the boil briefly over moderate heat.

PORK

• Trim off as much external fat as you can, and on tenderloins, use a small, sharp knife to remove the silver, pearlescent membrane covering its length.

• Lean cuts of pork benefit from a marinade or spice rub to add flavor that is lacking due to the absence of fat. Or, you can brush the pork with a little olive oil to prevent it drying out.

LAMB

• Trim off as much external fat as you can, as it can taste and smell unpleasant when charred.

• Cook lamb as you would beef. For the best flavor, do not cook it past medium.

• Allow lamb to rest after grilling, as you would beef.

• Serve hot, on warmed plates; cold lamb fat is unappealing.

POULTRY

• Remove any external fat.

• Removing the skin is optional. Leaving the skin on protects the delicate meat, keeps it juicier and adds flavor. Consider keeping the skin on during cooking and removing it afterward, if desired.

• Poultry should generally be cooked until opaque throughout (the exception is duck breasts; cook these until they are reddish pink). For bone-in cuts of poultry, make a small incision near the bone and check that no pink is visible.

• Skinless breast fillets are the easiest cut to grill. Marinate to give them more flavor and baste with oil during cooking to stop them drying out. For attractive cross-hatched grill marks, place the fillets on a hot grill rack for 2 minutes. Using tongs, rotate the breasts 90° and grill them for 2–4 minutes longer.

FISH AND SEAFOOD
• Trim off excess skin from fish fillets or steaks, and remove any small bones in fillets or steaks with needle-nose pliers.

• To grill a large whole fish, place lemon slices and herbs in the body cavity and wrap fish in oiled aluminum foil. Cook over direct heat on the grill.

• Clams, mussels and oysters should be well scrubbed before cooking. Discard any that are not tightly closed or that do not quickly close when touched.

KABOBS AND SATAYS
• Select lean meat and trim off any visible fat. Cut meat evenly into 1-inch (2.5-cm) cubes for kabobs or thin strips for satays. (Or, buy meat ready prepared from your butcher.)

• Use wooden or metal skewers, preferably with wooden handles. Wooden skewers must be soaked in water for about 30 minutes before use to prevent charring. Soaking the skewers also helps stop meat from falling off or rolling over while cooking; the wood swells when immersed in water and will shrink at the same rate as the food when it is cooking. Oil metal skewers to make it easy to remove the cooked meat.

• Slightly compact the meat (and vegetables, if using) to prevent the food rolling about. Closely packed ingredients take a little longer to cook.

• Cooking times are approximate and will vary according to the cut of meat, its thickness, how tightly packed it is on the skewers, and the type of grill you are using. Use the following as a guide:

Rare: Kabobs, 2–3 minutes each side; satays, 1–2 minutes each side.

Medium: Kabobs, 4–6 minutes each side; satays, 2–3 minutes each side.

Well done: Kabobs, 6–9 minutes each side; satays, 3–4 minutes each side.

How to Tell When Foods Are Done

Cooking times given in recipes are only guidelines. Variables such as the material and thickness of a pan, the heat of the coals or the wattage of a particular electric grill will greatly affect how quickly the food cooks.

It is important to check foods often; overcooked foods will be dry or tough, especially delicate foods, such as seafood, or lean foods, such as pork tenderloin. Undercooked foods, on the other hand—especially ground (minced) meats, pork products and chicken—can harbor dangerous microorganisms. Remember that foods continue to cook for a while after they are removed from the heat, so you can take them from the grill just before the desired degree of doneness has been reached.

Poultry should be opaque throughout, with no traces of pink in the flesh or juices. To check small pieces of poultry, make a small cut into the thickest part or pierce it with a long-handled fork. For larger pieces or whole birds, insert an instant-read thermometer into the thickest part (not touching bone); breast meat should be at least 170°F (77°C) and dark meat should be at least 180°F (82°C). Ground chicken or turkey patties should reach 165°F (74°C) in the center.

For beef, veal and lamb, make an incision into the thickest part to see if it has reached the desired degree of doneness. Rare meat will look reddish pink in the center; medium-rare will be light pink in the center; and medium will have just a trace of pink. Cooking meat beyond medium runs the risk of it being dry and tough. The exception is ground meat, which carries a higher risk of contamination, so should always be well done.

Another way to test meat is by pressing it with tongs. For rare meat, remove when sealed on both sides and the meat feels springy. For medium meat, after sealing both sides, reduce the heat to medium if using a grill pan. If using a wood or charcoal grill, move the meat to a cooler section of the grill. Continue cooking until it feels a little firmer, turning it twice at most.

You can also use an instant-read thermometer to check if meat is done. Insert the thermometer into the thickest part of a piece of meat, away from the bone. The United States Department of Agriculture (USDA) recommends that beef, veal and lamb should register 145°F (63°C) for

medium rare, 160°F (71°C) for medium and 170°F (77°C) for well done. Ground meat patties should register 160°F (71°C) in the center.

Pork should register 160°F (71°C) on the thermometer for medium and 170°F (77°C) for well done. For moist, tender results, a slight trace of rosiness should remain in the center.

Fish and other seafoods should not be overcooked or they will lose their delicate flavor and texture. For fish, insert a fork or the tip of a sharp knife at the thickest part to see if the fish is just losing its translucency and is just pulling apart into flakes.

For such shellfish as shrimp (prawns) and lobster tails, cook just until they are translucent throughout. Cook mussels, oysters and clams just until their shells open. Discard any whose shells do not open.

Vegetables are generally done when they can be easily pierced with a toothpick or wooden skewer. This is especially important for eggplant, which has an unpleasant astringent quality when undercooked.

The chart on pages 31–33 gives approximate grilling times for various foods and the chart on pages 36–37 shows indoor grilling times.

Type of food	Size/weight	Heat	Doneness	Cooking time (per side)
Meat				
Flank steak	3/4–1 inch (2–2.5 cm) thick	medium	medium-rare to medium	5–7 minutes
Other steak	1–2 inches (2.5–5 cm) thick	medium	rare to medium	5–12 minutes
Hamburgers	1–2 inches (2.5–5 cm) thick	medium	medium-rare to medium	5–12 minutes
Veal chops	1–1 1/2 inches (2.5–4 cm) thick	medium	medium to well done	9–15 minutes
Lamb chops	1–2 inches (2.5–5 cm) thick	medium	medium-rare to medium	5–10 minutes
Pork chops	3/4–1 1/2 inches (2–4 cm) thick	medium	medium (barely pink)	5–15 minutes
Pork cutlets	1/2 inch (1 cm) thick	medium-hot	medium (barely pink)	3–4 minutes
Pork tenderloin	10–12 oz (300–360 g)	medium	medium (barely pink)	12–15 minutes
Sausages, raw	4–6 oz (120–180 g)	medium	cooked through	6–8 minutes
Sausages, cooked	4–6 oz (120–180 g)	medium	heated through	2–3 minutes
Ham steak, fully cooked	1 inch (2.5 cm) thick	medium	heated through	10–12 minutes

GRILLING TIMES

Type of food	Size/weight	Heat	Doneness	Cooking time (per side)
Poultry				
Chicken pieces, bone-in	10 oz (300 g)	medium	opaque, no pink at bone	12–15 minute
Chicken breast, bone-in	10 oz (300 g)	medium	opaque, no pink at bone	10–12 minutes
Chicken breast fillets	4–5 oz (120–150 g)	medium	opaque throughout	6–8 minutes
Turkey breast cutlets	4–6 oz (120–180 g)	medium	opaque throughout	6–8 minutes
Duck breasts	4 oz (120 g)	medium	pink in center	5–6 minutes
Seafood				
Fish fillets	1/2–1 1/2 inches (1–4 cm)	medium	flesh just flakes	2–8 minutes
Whole fish	3/4–1 1/2 lb (360–720 g)	medium	flesh just flakes	6–15 minutes
Shrimp, medium	(16–20 per lb/480 g)	medium	opaque	2–4 minutes
Shrimp, jumbo	(12–15 per lb/480 g)	medium	opaque	3–6 minutes
Scallops, medium	(12–14 per lb/480 g)	medium	opaque	2–4 minutes
Lobster tails	1/2 lb (240 g)	medium	opaque	8–10 minutes
Oysters, clams, mussels	various	hot	until shells open	4–6 minutes (total)

Indoor Grilling Methods

Purists may argue that true barbecuing can only be done with a live fire, but apartment dwellers and those who like to barbecue year-round will argue for the convenience of indoor grilling. This method is fast, flavorful, healthful and, unlike outdoor grilling, it's independent of the weather or season.

The choice of machines, pans and range-top units for indoor grilling may seem confusing, but there are only two basic types: those that grill on one side at a time and those that grill on both sides at once. Grill pans, one-sided electric indoor grills and vented gas or electric grills that are part of a stovetop all cook the food with intense heat on one side at a time. Two-sided electric grills cook the food simultaneously from the top and bottom, cutting the cooking time in half. All of these indoor methods approximate the high-heat searing and charring so prized in outdoor grilling.

When choosing a piece of equipment, keep in mind that grill pans can be easier to store, but the smoke they produce requires a good exhaust system. Electric grills have a receptacle to catch any fat and juices that drip away, which makes them almost smoke free.

USING AND CARING FOR ELECTRIC GRILLS

Be sure to read the instructions that come with your particular machine. To protect the nonstick cooking surface, always use nylon or wooden utensils to maneuver foods or use metal tongs but be careful not to scratch the grill plates. Place the grill on a dry and level surface, with its cord safely out of the way and always unplug it when it is not in use.

Some machines have removable grill plates that can go in the sink or dishwasher for cleaning. If the plates are not removable, let the machine cool after cooking, then place it next to the sink and swab the cooking surfaces with hot soapy water. Let it stand for a few minutes so the baked-on particles soften, then wipe it clean with a wet sponge or cloth. Repeat with more hot soapy water as needed. Never immerse the machine.

USING AND CARING FOR GRILL PANS

Grill pans have a ridged surface, which allows the food to sit up off the bottom of the pan as the fat collects below. They may be square, rectangular or round, and can be made of cast iron, metal or enameled metal, often with a nonstick surface. A large

grill pan can accommodate more food, so is more versatile.

Cast-iron pans without a non-stick surface should be "seasoned" before using, to keep them from rusting and to prevent foods from sticking. To season a new cast-iron pan, scrub it in hot soapy water with a nylon or plastic brush or scrubber, then dry it completely. Rub it inside and out with solid vegetable shortening. Put the pan in a 300°F (150°C/Gas Mark 2) oven to bake for 15 minutes; remove the pan from the oven and carefully pour off any excess melted shortening. Return it to the oven and bake for 1 hour

longer. Let the pan cool slowly in the turned-off oven. After each use, clean the pan with hot soapy water, scrubbing if necessary; never put it in the dishwasher. Dry it with a towel and store it in a dry place to avoid rust.

You may want to brush the pan lightly with oil the first few times you use it; as it ages, it will develop a darker color and become increasingly "nonstick." Most other grill pans have a nonstick coating and do not require seasoning.

COOKING TIMES FOR INDOOR GRILLING

The following times are offered as guidelines only. Times will vary with individual electric grills, pans, and stoves, as well as the thickness of the food and how well cooked you want it to be. Test frequently, especially as the food approaches the desired degree of doneness.

Item	Electric grill	Grill pan
Chicken breast half, boneless and skinless, 4 oz (120 g)	4–5 minutes	8–10 minutes
Chicken breast half, bone-in	6–8 minutes	12–15 minutes
Chicken thighs, boneless	4–5 minutes	8–10 minutes
Chicken thighs, bone-in	8–10 minutes	15–20 minutes
Cut-up whole chicken	15–18 minutes	20–25 minutes
Chicken kabobs	2–3 minutes	4–6 minutes
Turkey breast cutlets	4 minutes	8–10 minutes
Duck breast, boneless, 6 oz (180 g)	4–6 minutes	8–12 minutes
Ground beef or poultry patties, 4 oz (120 g)	4–7 minutes	8–14 minutes
Beef steak, boneless, 1 inch (2.5 cm) thick	4–5 minutes for medium rare	8–10 minutes for medium rare
London broil, 1¼ inches (3 cm) thick	8 minutes for medium rare	18–20 minutes for medium rare
Beef or lamb kabobs	2–3 minutes for medium rare	4–6 minutes for medium rare

COOKING TIMES FOR INDOOR GRILLING

Item	Electric grill	Grill pan
Lamb chops, rib or loin, 1 inch (2.5 cm) thick	6–8 minutes for medium rare	10–14 minutes for medium rare
Whole pork tenderloin, 12 oz (360 g)	8 minutes	15 minutes
Country-style pork spareribs	10–12 minutes	18–20 minutes
Pork chops, rib or loin, 3/4–1 inch (2–2.5 cm) thick	6–8 minutes	12–15 minutes
Pork chops, rib or loin, 1/2 inch (1 cm) thick	3–4 minutes	6 minutes
Hot dogs	2 1/2–3 minutes	5–6 minutes
Scallops	2 1/2–4 minutes	5–8 minutes
Shrimp, large	2–3 minutes	5–8 minutes
Fish fillets or steaks	2–3 min per 1/2 inch (1 cm) of thickness	4–6 min per 1/2 inch (1 cm) of thickness
Potato slices, 1/4 inch (5 mm) thick	12–15 minutes	15–20 minutes, covered with foil
Bell peppers, sliced	4–5 minutes	8–10 minutes
Mushrooms, button	2–3 minutes	6–8 minutes
Mushrooms, portobello	3–4 minutes	6–8 minutes

Food Safety

Following the basic food safety hints below will ensure that you maintain good food hygiene and minimize the chances of disease transmission.

• While some cookbooks suggest marinating foods at room temperature or removing them from the refrigerator and allowing them to to warm to room temperature before grilling, this is not recommended by the USDA; bacterial growth occurs when food is above 40°F (4°C).

• Poultry can be marinated in the refrigerator, well-covered, for 1–2 days. Red meat can be marinated for 3–5 days.

Marinating in food-safe resealable plastic bags makes cleanup easy, but be sure to discard the bags after use.

• If a marinade is to be used subsequently for basting or as a sauce, boil it for a few minutes to destroy any bacteria from the raw ingredients. Never reuse a marinade for a new batch of raw food.

• Don't put cooked foods back on a cutting board or platter that has just held raw foods.

• Wash your hands before and after handling raw meat, poultry, fish and eggs.

• Remember that ground meats are particularly susceptible to bacterial contamination because of all the surfaces exposed during the grinding process. Always cook ground meats thoroughly—until there is no trace of pink in the center.

• When entertaining, don't leave cooked foods out at room temperature for more than 2 hours.

Butterflying a Whole Chicken

Butterflying chicken allows the maximum surface area to be exposed to the grill. Use the indirect-heat method of grilling for this type of chicken. A kettle-type barbecue is ideal. Marinating the chicken will add flavor and promote tenderness.

Using poultry or kitchen shears, cut closely along both sides of the backbone for the entire length of the chicken. Discard the backbone (or reserve, along with other trimmings, for stock).

Turn the bird skin-side up, place on a cutting board and open it out as flat as possible. Cover with plastic wrap. Strike the breast firmly in the center with the flat side of a meat mallet. (This breaks the breastbone so the bird lies flat.)

Twist wing tips under the back. Halfway between the legs and breastbone near the tip of the breast, cut a 1-inch (2.5-cm) slit through the skin on either side of and parallel with the breastbone. Insert the tips of the drumsticks into the slits.

Place the butterflied chicken into a large baking dish and marinate, or proceed as directed in the recipe.

The backbone, along with other chicken offcuts, can be kept for making stock.

STEP 1
Removing the Backbone
Set the bird on the cutting board breast-side down. With kitchen scissors or poultry shears, cut closely along one side of the backbone, then the other; discard backbone.

STEP 2
Flattening the Bird
Turn the chicken skin-side up with the breast facing you, wings up, legs down. Open the bird as flat as possible. Cover with a large sheet of plastic wrap. Flatten by striking the breast firmly in the center with the smooth side of a meat mallet to break the breastbone.

STEP 3
Tucking the Legs into Slits
Halfway between the legs and breastbone, near the bottom tip of the breast, cut a 1-inch (2.5-cm) slit through the loose skin on either side of and parallel with the breastbone. Insert the tips of the drumsticks into the slits to secure them so they won't pop up during grilling.

The Basics

Using Marinades

Marinades are an easy way to add extra flavor to meat, poultry and seafood. Those that contain an acidic ingredient, such as citrus juice, wine or vinegar, also help to tenderize the more inexpensive cuts of meat. The longer the marination time, the more tender and flavorsome the result. Eight hours or overnight gives the best results, but even 1 hour's marinating will be effective.

Choose marinade ingredients that complement the flavor of the dish you have chosen. Stronger-flavored meats can take robust marinades, but chicken and seafood need more subtle marinades to enhance, not overwhelm, their milder taste.

Mix the marinade ingredients. Place the meat, fish or poultry in a glass or ceramic dish or in a heavy-gauge lock-seal plastic bag. Add marinade, turning the meat to coat it well. (If the marinade contains an acidic ingredient, such as wine or citrus juice, don't use metal dishes; the acid will react with the metal dish and produce an unpleasant taste.) Place in the refrigerator.

Drain the meat before cooking it, but retain any leftover marinade; it can be used as a baste when the meat is cooking.

Marinades containing raw meat juices must be cooked thoroughly to kill the bacteria that could transmit disease. When basting with a marinade, cook it on the meat for at least 5 minutes after the last time the meat is basted. Alternatively, boil the marinade for a few minutes. It can then also be served as a dipping sauce, if desired.

When using a marinade that contains sugar or honey, cook the meat on a lower temperature than usual to prevent the marinade burning. You may need to increase the cooking time to compensate for the lower temperature.

STEPS FOR SCORING AND MARINATING FOOD

STEP 1

Scoring

Large or thick pieces of fish or meat (here, boneless chicken pieces) can be scored to allow the marinade to penetrate better. First remove any skin, if desired. Then, using a sharp knife, make shallow parallel marks in the meatiest section of each piece.

STEP 2

Marinating

Combine marinade ingredients in a small bowl, then transfer to a heavy-duty plastic bag large enough to hold all of the meat pieces. Add the meat, seal the bag, and turn several times to coat the meat. Lay the bag in a shallow bowl or baking dish. For marinating times longer than 30 minutes, or in hot weather, put the dish in the refrigerator.

STEP 3

Turning the Bag

As the chicken marinates, turn the bag several times so that the pieces are immersed in the marinade. This way the juices evenly penetrate all the pieces.

PART TWO

RECIPES

The following pages contain dozens of delicious
recipes for both outdoor and indoor grilling.
There are traditional barbecued meats and modern
interpretations, as well as delicious seafoods and
grilled vegetables. To accompany your
main course, there is also a range
of salads and desserts.

MARINADES, SAUCES AND CONDIMENTS

Marinades

For all of the following marinades, combine the ingredients for your chosen recipe in a nonreactive (that is, glass or china) bowl. Avoid metal bowls; metal may react with acidic ingredients such as citrus juice, producing an unpleasant flavor. Mix well. Place the chicken, seafood or fish in a shallow, nonreactive bowl or in a heavy-gauge lock-seal plastic bag and pour over the marinade. Stir or turn to coat the food well. Marinate, covered, for several hours or in the refrigerator overnight. Brush with marinade during cooking. See also pages 42–43 for general guidelines about marinating.

SATAY

1 small onion, grated

2 cloves garlic, crushed

1 teaspoon grated fresh ginger

1 cup (8 fl oz/240 ml) soy sauce

1/2 cup (4 fl oz/120 ml) coconut milk

1/4 cup (2 fl oz/60 ml) dry sherry

1/4 cup (2 fl oz/60 ml) sesame oil

3 tablespoons lime juice

1 tablespoon chili paste

2 tablespoons tamarind paste

Makes about 2 1/2 cups (20 fl oz/600 ml)

MEDITERRANEAN

3 cloves garlic, crushed

1/2 cup (4 oz/120 g) tomato paste

1/2 cup (4 fl oz/120 ml) olive oil

1/4 cup (2 fl oz/60 m) red wine

2 teaspoons dried oregano

Makes about 1 1/4 cups (10 fl oz/300 ml)

MARINADES

FIVE-SPICE

¼ cup (2 fl oz/60 ml) honey

¼ cup (2 fl oz/60 ml) dry sherry

¼ cup (2 fl oz/60 ml) soy sauce

2 teaspoons sesame oil

2 teaspoons Chinese five-spice powder

2 cloves garlic, finely chopped

2 teaspoons grated fresh ginger

Makes about 1 cup
(8 fl oz/240 ml)

BEER

4 cups (1 qt/960 ml) beer

1 cup (8 fl oz/240 ml) olive or safflower oil

1 cup (8 fl oz/240 ml) tomato sauce

½ cup (4 fl oz/120 ml) Dijon mustard

¼ cup (2 fl oz/60 ml) Worcestershire sauce

2 onions, chopped

2 cloves garlic, finely chopped

Makes about 6 cups
(48 fl oz/1.4 l)

HORSERADISH

1 tablespoon canola oil

1 tablespoon horseradish cream

½ cup (4 fl oz/120 ml) white wine

2 teaspoons chopped cilantro (fresh coriander)

2 teaspoons wholegrain mustard

Makes about ¾ cup
(6 fl oz/180 ml)

SPICY CITRUS

1⅓ cups (11 fl oz/330 ml) grapefruit juice

⅔ cup (5 fl oz/150 ml) orange juice

⅔ cup (5 fl oz/150 ml) olive oil (add a few drops sesame oil, optional)

2 cloves garlic, crushed

2 teaspoons hot paprika

2 tablespoons soft brown sugar or honey

Makes about 3 cups (24 fl oz/720 ml)

RED WINE AND MUSTARD

2½ cups (20 fl oz/600 ml) red wine

2 cups (16 fl oz/480 ml) olive oil

½ cup (4 fl oz/120 ml) port

¼ cup (2 fl oz/60 ml) balsamic vinegar

¼ cup (2 fl oz/60 ml) mustard

2 onions, peeled and sliced

2 garlic cloves, finely chopped

2 bay leaves, crumbled

Several sprigs parsley

2 tablespoons brown sugar

Several black peppercorns

Makes 6 cups (48 fl oz/1.4 l)

HONEY-MINT

1 teaspoon sesame oil

2 tablespoons fresh lemon juice

1–2 teaspoons seeded, finely chopped chili

2 tablespoons chopped fresh mint leaves

4 teaspoons honey

Makes about ⅓ cup (2½ fl oz/75 ml)

SPICY ASIAN-STYLE

1 cup (8 fl oz/240 ml) soy sauce

1 cup (8 fl oz/240 ml) plum sauce

1 cup (8 fl oz/240 ml) safflower oil

1/4 cup (2 fl oz/60 ml) oyster sauce

1/4 cup (2 fl oz/60 ml) lemon juice

1 tablespoon sesame oil

1 tablespoon grated fresh ginger

1 tablespoon chopped lemongrass

2 teaspoons chili oil

1 teaspoon five-spice powder

1 teaspoon ground coriander

2 cloves garlic, finely chopped

1 small chili, finely chopped

Makes 4 cups (32 fl oz/960 ml)

WINE AND HERB

1 1/2 cups (12 fl oz/360 ml) olive oil

1 cup (8 fl oz/240 ml) dry white wine

1/2 cup (4 fl oz/120 ml) dry vermouth

1/2 cup (4 fl oz/120 ml) lemon juice

2 cloves garlic, finely chopped

6 golden (French) shallots, chopped

2 tablespoons lemon thyme, crumbled

Several sprigs parsley

2 tablespoons chopped dill

1 lemon, sliced

Makes 4 cups (32 fl oz/960 ml)

GARLIC AND OREGANO

2 tablespoons olive oil

2 tablespoons dry white wine

4–6 teaspoons fresh oregano leaves or 2–3 teaspoons dried

6 large cloves garlic, crushed

Red pepper flakes or cayenne pepper

Makes 1/2 cup (4 fl oz/120 ml)

Right, top to bottom:
Texas Barbecue Sauce (page 61),
Mexican Spice Paste (page 54),
Horseradish Marinade (page 50),
Middle Eastern Spice Rub (page 55), Garlic and Oregano Marinade (page 52)

Spice Pastes and Rubs

MEXICAN SPICE PASTE

2 tablespoons mild chili powder

1 tablespoon hot chili powder

1 teaspoon salt

1 teaspoon ground cumin

1/2 teaspoon ground cinnamon

1/2 teaspoon ground coriander

1/8 teaspoon ground cloves

3 tablespoons olive oil or vegetable oil

2 tablespoons peanut butter

1 tablespoon fresh lime juice

2 teaspoons toasted (Asian) sesame oil

Fresh lime, cut into wedges, to serve

In a small bowl, whisk together the chili powders, salt, cumin, cinnamon, coriander and cloves.

Add the oil, peanut butter, lime juice and sesame oil and whisk until smooth. Store the paste tightly covered in the refrigerator for up to 1 week.

Brush generously over boneless chicken breasts, medallions of pork tenderloin or slices of turkey breast before grilling or barbecuing. Serve with wedges of fresh lime.

NOTE Peanuts and toasted sesame seeds often enrich Mexican dishes, and peanut butter and sesame oil are handy sources for those flavors.

Makes about 1/2 cup
(4 fl oz/120 ml)

MIDDLE EASTERN SPICE RUB

2 tablespoons ground cumin

4 teaspoons freshly ground black pepper

4 teaspoons ground turmeric

2 teaspoons ground cinnamon

2 teaspoons coarse salt

In a small dish, combine all the ingredients. Store in an airtight container at room temperature.

Brush evenly over meat before grilling or barbecuing.

Makes about ½ cup (4 oz/120 g)

VINDALOO PASTE

¼ cup (2 fl oz/60 ml) white vinegar

2 teaspoons ground cumin

2 teaspoons turmeric

2 teaspoons hot mustard, smooth or coarse-grain

1 teaspoon ground cardamom

1 teaspoon seeded and finely chopped red or green chili

1 teaspoon ground cinnamon

In a bowl, stir the ingredients together until smooth. Store the paste, tightly covered, in a jar in the refrigerator for up to 1 week.

Brush evenly over meat before grilling or barbecuing.

Makes about ½ cup (4 fl oz/120 ml)

Marinades, Sauces and Condiments

55

NORTH AFRICAN SPICE PASTE

2 cloves garlic, finely chopped

2 teaspoons grated fresh ginger

½ teaspoon salt

2 tablespoons olive oil

1 tablespoon paprika

1 teaspoon ground cumin

¼ teaspoon cayenne pepper

Few sprigs cilantro (fresh coriander) (optional), to serve

Using a mortar and pestle, combine the garlic, ginger and salt and mash to a paste. (Alternatively, use a chef's knife and a combination of chopping and mashing with the flat side of the knife to make the paste.)

Transfer the paste to a small bowl and add the oil, paprika, cumin and cayenne pepper. Stir together thoroughly. Store in an airtight container in the refrigerator for up to 1 week.

Brush generously over chicken, fish or lamb before grilling or barbecuing. Serve with fresh cilantro, if desired.

Makes about 3 tablespoons

Flavored Butters

CHILI AND GINGER

1 cup (8 oz/240 g) butter, softened

1 clove garlic, crushed

2 teaspoons chili oil

1 teaspoon chopped fresh chili

1 tablespoon grated ginger

2 teaspoons paprika

1 tablespoon tomato paste

Place all of the ingredients in the bowl of a food processor and process until combined. Spoon the butter into a serving dish and refrigerate until firm.

Makes about 1 1/4 cups (10 oz/300 g)

MUSTARD AND HORSERADISH

1 cup (8 oz/240 g) butter, softened

1 clove garlic, crushed

2 tablespoons seeded mustard

1 tablespoon horseradish cream

2 tablespoons chopped chives

1 tablespoon chopped fresh rosemary

Place the butter in the bowl of a food processor with the garlic, mustard and horseradish cream and process until combined.

Transfer to a bowl and stir in the chives and rosemary. Spoon the flavored butter into a serving dish and refrigerate until firm.

Makes about 1 1/4 cups (10 oz/300 g)

FLAVORED BUTTERS

HERB AND LIME

1 cup (8 oz/240 g) butter, softened

1 tablespoon grated lime zest (rind)

2 tablespoons lime juice

1 clove garlic, crushed

2 golden(French) shallots, chopped

2 tablespoons chopped parsley

2 tablespoons chopped chives

1 tablespoon chopped tarragon

Place the butter in the bowl of a food processor with the lime zest and juice, garlic, shallots and herbs, and process until combined. Spoon the flavored butter into a serving dish and refrigerate until firm.

Makes about 1¼ cups (10 oz/300 g)

Sauces and Ketchups

PEANUT SATAY SAUCE

1 cup (8 oz/240 g) crushed peanuts

1½ tablespoons olive oil

1 medium onion, finely chopped

1 clove garlic, finely chopped

2 teaspoons curry paste or powder

2 small red chilies, finely chopped

1 tablespoon soy sauce

1 tablespoon lemon juice

2 cups (16 fl oz/480 ml) water

Place the peanuts in the bowl of a food processor and process until finely chopped.

Heat the oil in a large heavy-based saucepan, add the onion and garlic and cook for 1 minute. Add the curry paste and cook until aromatic. Add the peanuts and cook for 2 minutes, stirring continuously.

Add the chilies, soy sauce, lemon juice and water. Bring to a boil and simmer uncovered for about 15 minutes.

Serve with chicken, beef or pork kabobs that have been marinated in satay marinade (page 48).

Makes about 2½ cups (20 fl oz/600 ml)

TEXAS BARBECUE SAUCE

2 teaspoons vegetable oil

1 small onion, finely diced

1 cup (8 fl oz/240 ml) ketchup

1/2 cup (4 fl oz/120 ml) brewed coffee

2 tablespoons molasses

2 tablespoons cider vinegar

2 tablespoons Worcestershire sauce

2 teaspoons Dijon mustard

1/2 teaspoon hot pepper sauce

In a small saucepan, heat the oil over medium heat. Add the onion and sauté until softened.

Add the remaining ingredients and stir well. Simmer over low heat for 30 minutes. Let cool. The sauce will keep, covered, in the refrigerator for up to 1 week.

Serve this classic sauce on meat, chicken or hamburgers, either as a baste or as a table sauce.

Makes about 1 1/2 cups (12 fl oz/360 ml)

SWEET CHILI AND GARLIC SAUCE

4 large cloves garlic

1 large red chili

1/2 cup (4 fl oz/120 ml) white vinegar

2/3 cup (5 oz/150 g) sugar

1/2 cup (5 oz/150 g) plum jam

1 tablespoon cornstarch (cornflour)

1 1/2 tablespoons water

In a food processor or blender, chop the garlic and chili. Transfer to a small saucepan and add the remaining ingredients.

Boil until smooth, stirring frequently. Cool, then pour into a tightly capped bottle.

NOTE This sauce will keep for several weeks in the refrigerator.

Makes about 1 1/2 cups (12 fl oz/360 ml)

Marinades, Sauces and Condiments

MEXICAN SAUCE

10 oz (300 g) ripe tomatoes

1 serrano chili, stem removed.

1 clove garlic, quartered

½ teaspoon salt, or to taste

2 tablespoons chopped cilantro
(fresh coriander)

Put the tomatoes and chili in a saucepan and add just enough water to cover. Boil until the tomato skins separate easily from the flesh, then drain and discard water.

Combine the tomatoes, chili and garlic in a food processor and process for a few seconds only; the sauce should be coarse.

Pour into a bowl, season with the salt and stir in the chopped cilantro. Serve immediately.

Makes about 1 cup
(8 fl oz/240 ml)

BASIL AND TOMATO SAUCE

6 tomatoes, skinned, seeded and quartered

3 tablespoons (1 1/2 fl oz/45 ml) vegetable oil

1/2 onion, sliced in half moons

2 allspice berries

2 black peppercorns

1/2 teaspoon salt, or to taste

1 bay leaf

1 sprig thyme

1 tablespoon fresh basil leaves, finely chopped

Chop the tomatoes coarsely in a food processor. Heat the oil in a saucepan and sauté the onion until translucent. Add the tomato, allspice, peppercorns and salt.

Cook over medium heat for 5 minutes, stirring occasionally. Add the bay leaf and thyme and simmer until the oil rises to the surface, about 10 minutes.

Before serving, remove the herbs and spices and discard. Add the basil and serve.

Makes 1 1/2 cups (12 fl oz/360 ml)

TRADITIONAL KETCHUP

5 lb (2.4 kg) ripe tomatoes, quartered

1/2 onion, roughly chopped

1 stick celery, roughly chopped

1 clove garlic, quartered

1/2 bay leaf

1/8 teaspoon celery seeds

1 small dried red chili

3/4 teaspoon mustard seeds

1 cup (8 fl oz/240 ml) Champagne vinegar or white wine vinegar

4 teaspoons honey

2 teaspoons molasses

In a food processor, process the tomatoes until smooth, about 1 minute, then pour into a large saucepan and set aside.

Process the onion, celery and garlic in the food processor, adding a few tablespoons of the processed tomatoes to facilitate puréeing.

Add the onion mixture to the saucepan containing the rest of the tomato mixture, then stir over medium heat for 5 minutes.

Place the bay leaf, celery seeds, chili and mustard seeds on a cheesecloth square, gather up all 4 corners, twist together and tie with string. Drop the bouquet garni into the tomato and onion mixture. Stir the vinegar, honey and molasses into the tomato and onion mixture and cook for 30 minutes. Remove the bouquet garni and discard.

Cook the ketchup for a further 10 minutes until thickened slightly. Stir occasionally to prevent the mixture catching on the bottom of the pan.

To remove any seeds, press the mixture through a strainer or food mill, if desired. Ladle the ketchup into a sterilized jar. Cap tightly, label if desired and refrigerate for up to 2 weeks.

Makes about 2 1/2 cups (20 fl oz/600 ml)

Marinades, Sauces and Condiments

CRANBERRY KETCHUP

12 oz (360 g) cranberries (fresh or thawed frozen)

1 large red (Spanish) onion, roughly chopped

1 cinnamon stick

½ teaspoon mustard seeds

½ teaspoon whole allspice

½ teaspoon black peppercorns

½ cup (4 fl oz/120 ml) water

1 cup (8 oz/240 g) sugar

½ cup (4 fl oz/120 ml) cider vinegar

1½ teaspoons salt

In a saucepan, just cover the cranberries and chopped onion with water and bring to a boil. Lower the heat, cover and simmer for 20 minutes.

Transfer the cranberry and onion mixture to a food processor and process until smooth. Test for smoothness; if there are any skins remaining, process again.

Spoon the mixture into the saucepan and cook over a medium heat for 20 minutes, until reduced to about 2 cups (16 fl oz/480 ml).

Place the cinnamon, mustard seeds, allspice and peppercorns in a square of cheesecloth (muslin) and tie with string. Add the spice bag, water, sugar, vinegar and salt to the mixture in the saucepan.

Cook slowly over a low heat until the mixture is very thick, 10–20 minutes. Stir frequently, being careful not to let the mixture burn. Use a pair of tongs to remove the spice bag from the saucepan and discard.

Ladle the ketchup into a sterilized jar. Cap tightly and label if desired. Refrigerate for up to 2 weeks.

Makes about 2 cups (16 fl oz/480 ml)

JALAPEÑO AND CRANBERRY SAUCE

1 lb (480 g) canned whole berry cranberry sauce

½ cup (4 fl oz/120 ml) apple jelly

1 jalapeño chili, finely chopped

In a saucepan, combine all of the ingredients. Cook slowly over low heat until the jelly melts, stirring all the while so the sauce does not burn. Pour into a sterilized container and refrigerate for up to 10 days.

Makes about 2 cups (16 fl oz/480 ml)

THAI BARBECUE SAUCE

1 teaspoon canola oil

1–2 teaspoons green curry paste

1 tablespoon chopped cilantro (fresh coriander) leaves

1 teaspoon Thai fish sauce

1 cup (8 fl oz/240 ml) coconut milk

Heat the oil in a saucepan over high heat. Add the green curry paste and fry until fragrant, about 1 minute.

Add the chopped cilantro, fish sauce and coconut milk. Stir well. Heat through over low heat and pour over grilled or barbecued chicken breasts or chicken or pork kabobs.

Makes about 1¼ cups (10 fl oz/300 ml)

TERIYAKI SAUCE

1 cup (8 fl oz/240 ml) Japanese soy sauce

1 cup (8 fl oz/240 ml) mirin (sweet Japanese rice wine)

1 tablespoon rice vinegar

1 tablespoon light brown sugar

4 teaspoons grated ginger

4 cloves garlic, crushed

Mix all of the ingredients together well. Cover and let stand for 2–3 hours before using. If stored in a sterilized jar, the mixture will keep in the refrigerator for 2–3 weeks.

Makes 2 cups (16 fl oz/480 ml)

Dips and Salsas

SMOOTH RED SALSA

2 tablespoons vegetable oil

1 small yellow onion, thinly sliced

2 cloves garlic, thinly sliced

1 jalapeño chili, stemmed, seeded and thinly sliced

1 teaspoon salt

1½ cups (12 fl oz/360 g) canned plum tomatoes, with juice

In a saucepan, heat the oil over medium heat. Add the onion and cook, stirring occasionally, until softened, about 10 minutes. Add the garlic, jalapeño and salt and cook for 2 minutes more.

Add the tomatoes with their juice, reduce the heat to low and continue cooking, stirring occasionally, until the tomatoes are soft and the liquid has reduced by half.

Let the mixture cool slightly, then transfer it to a blender and purée until smooth.

Set a strainer over a bowl and pour the mixture through. Serve warm or at room temperature.

Store tightly covered in the refrigerator for up to 4 days or in the freezer for up to 1 month.

NOTE This is not the usual chunky tomato salsa, but a smoother, more sophisticated sauce. It may be served warm or at room temperature, as a table salsa or as a topping for simple grilled chicken or fish.

Makes about 1 cup (8 fl oz/240 ml)

GUACAMOLE

3 ripe avocados

1 fresh jalapeño chili, stemmed, seeded and finely chopped

½ white onion, diced

¼ cup (⅓ oz/10 g) coarsely chopped cilantro (fresh coriander) leaves

Juice of 1 lime

½ teaspoon salt

Freshly ground black pepper

1 ripe tomato, seeded and diced (optional)

Cut each avocado lengthwise into quarters, removing the pit. Peel off the skin and place the pulp in a bowl. Using a potato masher, spoon or your hand, mash lightly. Add the jalapeño, onion, cilantro, lime juice, salt, pepper to taste and the diced tomato, if desired. Mix just until combined; chunks of avocado should remain visible.

To serve, spoon the guacamole into a serving bowl or onto a plate. If not serving immediately, poke the avocado pits down into the center of the mixture (this helps stop the avocado from discoloring), cover tightly with plastic wrap and refrigerate for up to 4 hours. Serve chilled with tortilla chips, if desired.

Makes about 2½ cups (20 oz/600 g)

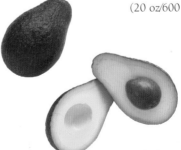

Marinades, Sauces and Condiments

BASIL PESTO

2 cups (2 oz/60 g) fresh basil
(or parsley, tarragon or
cilantro/fresh coriander)

3 cloves garlic, quartered

½ cup (4 fl oz/120 ml) olive oil

Salt to taste

¾ cup (3 oz/90 g) freshly grated
Parmesan cheese

2 tablespoons butter

3 tablespoons pine nuts

Place the fresh herbs in a food
processor, add the garlic, drizzle
in the oil (reserving 1 teaspoon)
and purée until smooth. Add
salt to taste.

Add the Parmesan cheese, butter
and pine nuts and process until
smooth. Pour into a sterilized jar
and cover with a thin layer of
olive oil.

Alternatively, you can freeze
the pesto in individual blocks in
an ice cube tray. When frozen,
transfer to a plastic bag and seal.

Makes about 2 cups
(1 lb/480 g)

Marinades, Sauces and Condiments

CILANTRO PESTO WITH NUTS

¼ cup (2 oz/60 g) butter

3 tablespoons unsalted roasted peanuts

½ cup (½ oz/15 g) loosely packed cilantro (fresh coriander) leaves

½ jalapeño chili, chopped

¾ cup (6 fl oz/180 ml) peanut oil

¼ cup (1 oz/30 g) freshly grated Parmesan cheese

Salt to taste

Purée the butter and peanuts in a food processor. Add the cilantro and chili and process.

Drizzle in the oil a drop at a time. Add the Parmesan and process again. Season with salt and process again.

Transfer to a dish or storage jar. The pesto will keep for 1–2 days in the refrigerator.

Makes about 1 cup (8 oz/240 g)

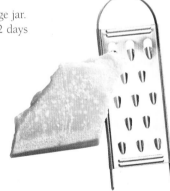

Marinades, Sauces and Condiments

MEXICAN SALSA

6 ripe tomatoes

2 jalapeño chilies, seeded and chopped

4 sprigs oregano

1/2 medium onion, finely chopped

1/4 cup (1/4 oz/7 g) chopped cilantro (fresh coriander)

2 cloves garlic, finely chopped

Salt to taste

Put the tomatoes in a hot skillet to crack the skins. Cook for 2–4 minutes to reduce the tomato juice slightly.

Cool, then remove the skins. Finely chop the tomatoes. In a bowl, combine the remaining ingredients with the tomatoes, mixing well. Spoon the salsa into a sterilized jar.

Cover securely and label, if desired. Keep for 3–5 days in the refrigerator.

Makes about 2 cups (1 lb/480 g)

TOMATILLO SALSA

3 jalapeño chilies, halved and seeded

1 medium onion, quartered

1 clove garlic, quartered

2 tablespoons finely chopped cilantro (fresh coriander)

20 tomatillos, husked, washed and heated until tender (to make 2½ cups/20 oz/600 g)

½ teaspoon sugar

Salt and pepper, to taste

2 tablespoons olive oil

In a food processor, finely chop the chilies, onion and garlic. Add the cilantro, tomatillos, sugar, salt and pepper and process until smooth. In a saucepan, heat the olive oil and add the puréed ingredients.

Cook over a medium heat for about 5 minutes, being careful not to burn.

Transfer the salsa to a serving bowl; if not using immediately, cover and store in the refrigerator for 6–7 days.

Makes about 3 cups (1½ lb/720 g)

TRADITIONAL TOMATO SALSA

4 large ripe tomatoes, roughly chopped

3 jalapeño chilies, halved and seeded

6–8 green (spring) onions, chopped

2 cloves garlic, quartered

8 sprigs cilantro (fresh coriander), stems removed

Salt to taste

In a food processor, process the tomatoes, chilies, onions, garlic and cilantro to a coarse texture. Stir in the salt, mixing well, and serve immediately or store, as is, in the refrigerator for 2 days. If there is any left over, transfer to a skillet and simmer for 5 minutes. This will allow the salsa to be kept longer.

Place in a storage container, and keep in the refrigerator for up to 1 week.

Makes about 2 cups (1 lb/480 g)

QUICK TOMATO SALSA

4 large ripe tomatoes, seeded and roughly chopped

2 fresh serrano chilies, stemmed and coarsely chopped

1/4 cup (2 fl oz/60 ml) fresh lime juice

1 teaspoon salt

1/2 teaspoon freshly ground black pepper

In a food processor, combine all the ingredients. Process to the desired texture.

Makes about 2 cups (1 lb/480 g)

MEAT AND POULTRY

Grilled Five-Spice Chicken

2 small chickens, about 2 lb (960 g) each

FIVE-SPICE MARINADE

1 piece fresh ginger, about 1 inch (2.5 cm) long, peeled and grated

4 cloves garlic, chopped

2 purple (Asian) shallots, chopped

1½ tablespoons brown sugar

½ teaspoon salt

¼ teaspoon ground pepper

½ teaspoon five-spice powder

2 tablespoons Vietnamese or Thai fish sauce

2 tablespoons soy sauce

1 tablespoon dry sherry

DIPPING SAUCE

1 clove garlic, very finely chopped

1 fresh small red chili, seeded and finely chopped

¼ cup (2 oz/60 g) sugar

¼ cup (2 fl oz/60 ml) fresh lime juice, including the pulp

5 tablespoons Vietnamese or Thai fish sauce

½ cup (4 fl oz/120 ml) water

Cut each chicken in half through the breast and backbone. Press down on the breasts to flatten the halves slightly.

For the marinade, combine the ginger, garlic, shallots, brown

sugar and salt in a mortar, blender or mini food processor. Mash with a pestle or process to a smooth paste. Transfer to a large shallow bowl. Add the pepper, five-spice powder, fish sauce, soy sauce and sherry. Stir well. Add the chicken halves and turn to coat with the marinade. Cover and let marinate in the refrigerator for a few hours or as long as overnight.

For the dipping sauce, in a mortar, mash together the garlic, chili and sugar with a pestle to form a paste. Add the lime juice and pulp, fish sauce and water and stir to dissolve the sugar. Strain the sauce into a bowl or jar and use immediately, or cover tightly and refrigerate for up to 5 days.

Prepare a fire in a charcoal grill. When the coals are ash white, place the chicken halves, bone side down, on the grill rack about 4 inches (10 cm) above the coals. Grill for 20 minutes. Turn the chicken over and continue to grill until cooked through and golden brown, about 20 minutes longer.

Serve hot with the dipping sauce.

Serves 4

Chicken with Tomato–Mint Pesto

1/3 cup (1/2 oz/15 g) packed fresh mint leaves

1/3 cup (1/2 oz/15 g) packed fresh parsley (stems removed)

1/3 cup (1 oz/30 g) drained, oil-packed, sun-dried tomatoes

1/4 cup (2 fl oz/60 ml) olive oil

1 clove garlic, halved

1 1/2 teaspoons finely grated lemon zest

1/4 teaspoon salt

1/8 teaspoon lemon–pepper seasoning

4 small chicken breast halves, about 1 1/4 lb (600 g) total

For the pesto, in a blender container or food processor bowl, combine the mint, parsley, tomatoes, olive oil, garlic, lemon zest, salt and lemon–pepper seasoning. Blend or process until finely chopped.

If desired, remove skin from chicken. Place a chicken breast half on the cutting board skin-side up. With a small knife or boning knife, make a pocket 2 inches (5 cm) deep and about 3 inches (7.5 cm) long in the breastbone side of the meat. Fill each pocket with one fourth of the pesto.

Prepare a fire in a charcoal grill. When the coals are ash white, place the chicken breasts on the grill rack about 4 inches (10 cm) above the coals. Grill for 15 minutes. Turn the chicken over and continue to grill until cooked through and golden brown, 10–15 minutes longer.

Serves 4

Middle Eastern Lamb Skewers

MARINADE

2 small onions, grated

¾ cup (6 fl oz/180 ml) olive oil

1 teaspoon ground black pepper

1 teaspoon dried oregano

1 teaspoon ground cinnamon

1 teaspoon ground cumin

Pinch of cayenne pepper

SKEWERS

1 lb (480 g) boneless leg of lamb, trimmed and cut into 1½-inch (4-cm) cubes

1 large red (Spanish) onion, cut into 1-inch pieces

4 plum (Roma) tomatoes, halved lengthwise and crosswise

2 small green bell peppers, cored and cut into 1½-inch (4-cm) pieces

¼ cup (2 fl oz/60 ml) olive oil

Salt and ground black pepper

Minted Yogurt Sauce (page 186) or purchased or homemade tzatziki, to serve (optional)

For the marinade, in a shallow, nonaluminum dish, combine all the marinade ingredients and mix well. Add the lamb and turn to coat well. Cover the dish and refrigerate for 8–24 hours.

Preheat a ridged grill pan according to the manufacturer's instructions.

Thread the lamb cubes alternating with the red onion onto skewers, leaving a little space between the pieces. Discard the used marinade.

On separate skewers, thread the tomato pieces alternating with the bell pepper pieces. Brush vegetable skewers with oil and season with salt and pepper.

Grill the vegetable skewers until the vegetables are tender and browned in spots, about 10 minutes, turning once midway through cooking time. Transfer to a platter; keep warm.

Grill the lamb skewers, in batches if necessary, until done to your liking, 6–8 minutes for medium-rare, turning once midway through cooking time.

Transfer the lamb skewers to the same platter as the vegetable skewers, arrange attractively, and serve immediately with the yogurt sauce or tzatziki, if liked.

Serves 4

Butterflied Citrus Chicken

⅓ cup (2½ fl oz/75 ml) olive oil or vegetable oil

⅓ cup (2½ fl oz/75 ml) orange juice

¼ cup (2 fl oz/60 ml) lemon juice

1½ teaspoons dried rosemary, crushed

2 cloves garlic, minced

½ teaspoon salt

¼ teaspoon pepper

2½–3 lb (1.2–1.4 kg) whole broiler-fryer (roasting) chicken, butterflied (page 40)

In a small bowl, stir together the oil, orange juice, lemon juice, rosemary, garlic, salt and pepper. Pour into a large plastic bag; add the chicken. Seal the bag and turn it to coat the chicken with the marinade. Marinate in the refrigerator for 8–24 hours, turning bag occasionally. Drain the marinade from the chicken, reserving marinade.

In a covered grill, arrange medium–hot coals around a drip pan, then test for medium heat (see page 20) above the pan, not over the coals. Place the chicken, skin-side up, on the grill rack directly over the drip pan, not over the coals.

Brush the chicken with some of the reserved marinade. Cover and grill for 30 minutes. Brush with additional marinade. Grill for 30–40 minutes more, or until the chicken is tender and no pink remains. Discard the remaining marinade.

Serves 4

Japanese Chicken Kabobs

MARINADE

1 cup (8 fl oz/240 ml) orange juice

2/3 cup (5 fl oz/150 ml) dry sherry

1/2 cup (4 fl oz/120 ml) soy sauce

4 teaspoons sugar

2 teaspoons grated orange zest

1 1/2 teaspoons grated fresh ginger

2 cloves garlic, finely chopped

CHICKEN

1 1/4 lb (600 g) boneless, skinless chicken breasts, cut into 1-inch (2.5-cm) cubes

6 green (spring) onions, cut into 1 1/2-inch (4-cm) pieces

For the marinade, in a small bowl, combine the orange juice, sherry, soy sauce, sugar, orange zest, ginger and garlic. Reserve 2/3 cup (5 fl oz/160 ml) and pour the rest into a shallow glass or china baking dish.

Thread the chicken onto skewers alternating with the green onions, leaving a little space between the pieces. Place in the marinade and turn to coat. Let stand at room temperature for 30 minutes, turning the skewers from time to time.

Meanwhile, put the reserved marinade in a small saucepan and simmer for 5 minutes, until thickened slightly. Set aside.

Preheat a two-sided electric indoor grill or ridged grill pan according to the manufacturer's instructions.

Remove the skewers from the marinade, shaking off the excess. Discard the used marinade.

If using the two-sided grill, place the skewers on the grill, close the cover, and cook, in batches if necessary, until the chicken is no longer pink in the center, 2–3 minutes.

If using the grill pan, cook the skewers in batches until chicken is no longer pink in the center, 4–6 minutes, turning once midway through cooking time.

Arrange the skewers on a platter, brush with the reserved cooked marinade, and serve immediately.

Serves 4

Croque-Monsieur

8 slices dense-textured white sandwich bread

½ cup (4 oz/120 g) unsalted butter, at room temperature

10 oz (300 g) Gruyère cheese, thinly sliced

5 oz (150 g) cooked ham, thinly sliced

Cornichons (French-style pickles)

Dijon mustard

Serves 4

Lightly coat one side of each bread slice with some of the butter. Layer half of the Gruyère slices on the unbuttered side of 4 bread slices. Top with the ham, dividing it evenly. Top the ham with the remaining Gruyère, again dividing it evenly. Top the cheese with the remaining bread slices, buttered sides up.

Preheat a two-sided electric indoor grill or ridged grill pan according to the manufacturer's instructions.

If using the two-sided grill, place one sandwich on the grill, close the cover, and cook until golden brown on both sides and the cheese melts, about 2 minutes. Transfer to a warmed platter and repeat with the remaining sandwiches.

If using the grill pan, slip one sandwich into the pan and cook until the bottom is golden brown, 1½–2 minutes. Using a spatula, turn the sandwich over and continue to cook, reducing the heat slightly, until golden brown on the bottom and the cheese melts, about 2 minutes longer. Transfer to a warmed platter and repeat with the remaining sandwiches.

If necessary, the sandwiches can be reheated for 2–3 minutes in a preheated 350°F (180°C) oven.

Serve with cornichons and Dijon mustard on the side.

Tarragon–Lemon Chicken Breasts

4 boneless chicken breasts, each about 5 oz (155 g)

Juice of 1 lemon

2 tablespoons vegetable oil

½ teaspoon white pepper

2 teaspoons dried tarragon

Sprigs of fresh tarragon, to serve

Lemon slices, to serve

Skin the chicken breasts and place in a glass dish. Mix the lemon juice, oil, pepper and dried tarragon together in a screwtop jar and shake vigorously to emulsify. Pour over the chicken and marinate for 20 minutes.

Prepare a fire in a charcoal grill or preheat a gas grill to medium heat. Cook the chicken over moderate heat until just cooked through, turning once. Test by pressing the thickest part: it should feel firm. Transfer to warmed serving plates. Garnish with sprigs of fresh tarragon and lemon slices.

NOTE The chicken can be marinated in the refrigerator, covered, for several hours in advance, if necessary.

Serves 4

Grilled Veal Chops with Salad

VEAL CHOPS

4 bone-in veal loin chops, about
½ lb (240 g) each

2 cloves garlic, halved lengthwise

Ground black pepper

4 teaspoons extra virgin olive oil

SALAD

1 small bunch arugula (rocket)

2 radicchio (red chicory) leaves,
sliced into thin shreds

4 Belgian endive (chicory/witloof)
leaves, sliced into thin shreds

2 small artichokes, trimmed (raw
or thawed, frozen), optional

1 oz (30 g) Parmesan cheese

4 lemon wedges

Extra virgin olive oil

Prepare a fire in a charcoal grill.

Using a sharp knife, slash the fat along the edge of each chop in 3 places to avoid curling during cooking. Place each chop between 2 sheets of plastic wrap and, using a meat mallet, pound ½ inch (1 cm) thick. Rub each chop all over with half of a garlic clove, pepper to taste and 1 teaspoon olive oil. Let stand at room temperature for 1 hour.

Arrange chops on a grill rack over hot coals. Cook, turning once, until done to your liking. For rare, cook 2–3 minutes on the first side and 1–2 minutes on the second; for medium, cook 4–5 minutes on the first side and 3–4 minutes on the second; for well-done, cook 6–7 minutes on the first side and 5–6 minutes on the second.

Transfer the chops to warmed individual plates and scatter an equal amount of arugula, radicchio and endive over the top of each chop. Thinly slice the artichokes lengthwise, if using, and scatter over the salad. Using a sharp knife or vegetable peeler, shave off paper-thin slices of the Parmesan cheese and scatter over the greens. Place a lemon wedge on each plate and pass the olive oil for drizzling over the top.

Serves 4

Thai Beef Salad

BEEF

2 cloves garlic

2 tablespoons finely chopped cilantro (fresh coriander)

1½ teaspoons sugar

1 teaspoon ground black pepper

2 tablespoons soy sauce

1 tablespoon Thai or Vietnamese fish sauce

1 tablespoon peanut or corn oil

1 lb (480 g) boneless sirloin steak

VINAIGRETTE AND SALAD

2 cloves garlic, minced

2 small fresh red or green chilies, chopped

1½ tablespoons sugar

¼ cup (2 fl oz/60 ml) Thai or Vietnamese fish sauce

⅓ cup (3 fl oz/80 ml) fresh lime juice

6 large red lettuce leaves, torn into pieces

3 small firm tomatoes, cut into wedges

1 small red onion, thinly sliced

1 small cucumber, peeled and thinly sliced

2 tablespoons coarsely chopped cilantro (fresh coriander), plus whole leaves for garnish

2 tablespoons coarsely chopped fresh mint

For the beef, combine garlic, cilantro, sugar and pepper in a mortar. Using a pestle, mash to a paste. Add the soy sauce, fish sauce and oil. Place the beef in a shallow dish and rub the mixture over both sides. Marinate for 1 hour at room temperature or cover and refrigerate for up to 4 hours.

For the vinaigrette, combine the garlic and chilies in a mortar. Using a pestle, mash to a paste. Stir in the sugar, fish sauce and lime juice. Set aside.

Preheat a two-sided electric indoor grill or ridged grill pan according to the manufacturer's instructions.

If using the two-sided grill, place beef on the grill, close the cover, and cook until done to your liking, 4–5 minutes for medium-rare. Set aside to cool.

If using the grill pan, cook until done to your liking, 8–10 minutes for medium-rare, turning it once midway through the cooking time. Set aside to cool.

In a large bowl, combine the salad ingredients and 2½ tablespoons of vinaigrette. Thinly slice beef across the grain and toss with the remaining vinaigrette. Divide salad and beef among 4 plates. Garnish with cilantro leaves and serve immediately.

Serves 4

Bacon-Wrapped Chicken Drumsticks

8 chicken drumsticks

½ teaspoon salt

½ teaspoon pepper

I small clove garlic, mashed (optional)

8 slices (rashers) bacon

I tablespoon vegetable oil

½ cup (4 oz/120 g) plum jam

I tablespoon cider vinegar, or to taste

I tablespoon mild chili sauce, or to taste

Prepare a fire in a charcoal grill or preheat a gas grill to medium–high heat.

Rub the drumsticks with the salt, pepper and garlic, if using. Wrap a slice of bacon firmly around each drumstick, securing the ends with toothpicks.

Brush with the vegetable oil and grill until cooked through, about 12 minutes. Turn frequently, brushing with additional oil. To test if done, pierce in the thickest part with a thin skewer; the juices should run clear.

For the sauce, heat the jam, cider vinegar and chili sauce in a small pan or microwave oven and mix well. Arrange the hot drumsticks on a platter around a dish of the sauce for dipping.

NOTE The drumsticks can be prepared in advance, wrapped in plastic wrap and refrigerated or frozen until needed. The sauce can be made several days in advance and refrigerated.

Serves 4

Butterflied Lamb with Couscous

1 leg of lamb, about 8½ lb (4.1 kg), boned and butterflied (about 6½ lb/3.1 kg boned)

¼ cup (2 fl oz/60 ml) extra virgin olive oil

1 tablespoon chopped garlic

2 teaspoons salt

2 teaspoons cracked pepper

1½ teaspoons chopped fresh rosemary

Grated zest and juice of 1 lemon

COUSCOUS

4 cups (28 oz/840 g) couscous

4 cups (32 fl oz/960 ml) chicken stock or water

⅔ cup (4 oz/120 g) diced red bell pepper (capsicum)

1 teaspoon saffron threads

1 teaspoon chopped garlic

1 teaspoon salt

1 oz (30 g) chopped green (spring) onions

2 oz (60 g) dried currants

1½ oz (45 g) pine nuts, toasted

1 tablespoon chopped fresh mint

2 tablespoons extra virgin olive oil

Fresh mint sprigs, for garnish

BUTTERFLIED LAMB WITH COUSCOUS

Place the lamb in a large glass or china dish. In a small bowl, combine the olive oil, garlic, salt, pepper, rosemary and lemon zest and juice. Drizzle the mixture over the lamb and rub it in well. Cover and refrigerate for at least 3 hours, or as long as overnight. About 1 hour before cooking, remove from refrigerator and bring to room temperature.

Prepare a fire in a charcoal grill using hardwood charcoal such as mesquite or hickory.

Place couscous in a heatproof bowl. In a small saucepan over high heat, combine the chicken stock or water, bell pepper, saffron, garlic and salt; bring to

a boil. Pour over the couscous, stir to combine, then cover with aluminum foil. Let stand for 8 minutes. Using a fork, fluff to break the couscous into individual grains. Cover again and let rest 5 minutes longer.

Add the green onions, currants, pine nuts, mint and olive oil and toss well to combine.

When the coals have burned down to a gray ash, place the lamb on the grill rack with the outside of the leg facing down. Grill for about 15 minutes. Turn over and grill until dark brown and done to your liking. Transfer to a large platter and let rest in a warm place for 5 minutes.

Serve the couscous at room temperature or briefly reheat in the microwave oven or in a large nonstick frying pan over high heat, tossing frequently, for 1–2 minutes. Thinly slice lamb across the grain and arrange on individual plates atop a mound of the couscous. Garnish with mint sprigs, if desired, and serve.

Serves 8 to 10

Steak Kabobs

MARINADE

¼ cup (2 fl oz/60 ml) olive oil

1 tablespoon fresh lemon juice

6 cloves garlic, sliced

KABOBS

1 lb (480 g) boneless sirloin steak, cut into 1¼-inch (3-cm) cubes

2 bunches green (spring) onions, cut into 2-inch (5-cm) lengths

16 cherry tomatoes

Salt and ground black pepper

For the marinade, in a small bowl, whisk together the oil, lemon juice, and garlic. Place the steak cubes in a large resealable plastic bag or shallow, nonaluminum dish; pour in the marinade and toss to coat the meat. If using a dish, cover with plastic wrap. Refrigerate for 1–2 hours.

Remove the meat from the marinade, shaking off any excess. Thread the cubes onto skewers, alternating them with pieces of green onion and tomatoes, leaving a little space between the pieces. Season on all sides with salt and pepper.

Preheat a large two-sided electric indoor grill or ridged grill pan according to the manufacturer's instructions.

If using the two-sided grill, place the kabobs on the grill, close the cover, and cook, in batches if necessary, until done to your liking, 2–3 minutes for medium-rare.

If using the grill pan, cook, in batches if necessary, until done to your liking, 4–6 minutes for medium-rare. Turn kabobs once midway through the cooking time. Serve immediately.

Serves 4

Rack of Lamb with Ratatouille

1 rack of lamb with 8 chops, about 3 lb (1.4 kg), bones frenched (see glossary)

3 tablespoons extra virgin olive oil

1 tablespoon chopped garlic

2 teaspoons coarsely chopped fresh rosemary

1 1/4 teaspoons salt

1/2 teaspoon ground black pepper

RATATOUILLE

1/2 cup (4 fl oz/125 ml) extra virgin olive oil

2 cups (7 oz/210 g) sliced yellow onions

3 cloves garlic, thinly sliced

3 zucchini (courgettes), cut crosswise into pieces 1/2 inch (10 mm) thick

1 eggplant (aubergine), peeled, quartered lengthwise and sliced crosswise into pieces 1/2 inch (10 mm) thick

2 red bell peppers (capsicums), seeded, deribbed and cut into large pieces

2 1/2 cups (15 oz/450 g) diced plum (Roma) tomatoes

3 fresh sprigs basil, chopped

1 1/2 teaspoons salt

1/2 teaspoon ground black pepper

2 tablespoons chopped fresh flat-leaf (Italian) parsley

Place the lamb in a shallow nonaluminum container and rub all over with the olive oil, garlic, rosemary, salt and pepper. Cover and refrigerate for at least 3 hours, or as long as overnight.

For the ratatouille, in a heavy frying pan over medium heat, warm the oil. Add the onion and sauté until translucent, about 5 minutes. Add the garlic and cook for 2–3 minutes. Add the zucchini, eggplant and bell peppers and cook, stirring, until heated through, about 5 minutes more. Stir in the tomato, basil, salt and pepper. Cover, reduce the heat to low and cook until tender, about 30 minutes.

Uncover the pan; the mixture should still be quite liquid. Cook until the mixture thickens, another 15–20 minutes. Remove from the heat, let cool briefly and stir in the parsley. Set aside. (At this point, the ratatouille can be covered and refrigerated for up to 3 days.)

Before the ratatouille is done, prepare a fire in a charcoal grill using hardwood charcoal such as mesquite or hickory.

When the coals have burned down to a gray ash, place lamb on the grill with the convex side of the bones facing down. Cook for 6–8 minutes, turn, cook for another 6–8 minutes, turn one

more time and cook for a final 2–3 minutes for medium-rare. To test if done, make an incision in the underside. If underdone, cook a few minutes more on each side. Transfer to a cutting board and let rest for 5 minutes in a warm spot.

While the lamb is cooking, if necessary, reheat the ratatouille in a saucepan over medium-high heat until heated through, 8–10 minutes.

Cut the rack into 2-bone portions and serve at once, accompanied with some of the ratatouille.

Serves 4

Spicy Spanish Kabobs

MARINADE

¼ cup (2 fl oz/60 ml) canola oil

3 tablespoons fresh lemon juice

2 tablespoons chopped fresh parsley

½ teaspoon paprika

½ teaspoon ground cumin

½ teaspoon salt

¼ teaspoon ground black pepper

¼ teaspoon cayenne pepper

Pinch of saffron (optional)

KABOBS

8 boneless, skinless chicken thighs, trimmed of fat and cut into 1-inch (2.5-cm) cubes

Lemon wedges, for garnish

For the marinade, in a medium bowl, whisk together the oil, lemon juice, parsley, paprika, cumin, salt, black pepper, cayenne and saffron, if using. Add the chicken and stir to coat. Cover with plastic wrap and marinate in the refrigerator for 4–24 hours, turning occasionally.

Preheat a two-sided electric indoor grill or ridged grill pan according to the manufacturer's instructions.

If using the two-sided grill, thread the marinated chicken onto skewers, leaving a little space between the pieces. Place the skewers on the grill, close the cover, and cook, in batches if necessary, until the chicken is no longer pink in the center, about 4 minutes.

If using the grill pan, thread the marinated chicken onto skewers, leaving a little space between the pieces. Cook, in batches if necessary, until the chicken is no longer pink in the center, about 6 minutes, turning once midway through the cooking time.

Serve with lemon wedges.

Serves 4

Firecracker Chicken Thighs

2 tablespoons sesame seeds, toasted until golden

1/4 cup (1 1/4 oz/40 g) finely chopped green (spring) onions

4 large cloves garlic, finely chopped

2–3 tablespoons hot bean paste or sauce (see glossary)

2 tablespoons soy sauce

1 tablespoon sesame oil

1 tablespoon sugar

1/8 teaspoon ground black pepper

6 bone-in chicken thighs, skin and excess fat removed

For the marinade, place the sesame seeds in a mortar and crush with a pestle. Transfer to a bowl and add the green onions, garlic, bean paste or sauce, soy sauce, sesame oil, sugar, and pepper; stir together well.

Score the meat on both sides of the chicken thighs with shallow diagonal cuts about 1 inch (2.5 cm) apart. Add the chicken to the marinade and turn to coat well. Cover and refrigerate for 4–24 hours, turning chicken occasionally.

Preheat a two-sided electric indoor grill or ridged grill pan according to the manufacturer's instructions.

Remove chicken from marinade, shaking off the excess.

If using the two-sided grill, place the chicken on the grill, close the cover, and cook, in batches if necessary, until the chicken is no longer pink in the center, 8–10 minutes.

If using the grill pan, cook, in batches if necessary, until the chicken is no longer pink in the center, 15–20 minutes, turning it once midway through the cooking time.

Serves 2 to 3

Grilled Reuben Sandwich

SPREAD

½ cup (4 oz/120 g) mayonnaise (regular or reduced fat)

2 tablespoons ketchup (tomato sauce)

2 tablespoons very finely chopped red (Spanish) onion

2 tablespoons very finely chopped dill pickle

2 tablespoons very finely chopped fresh parsley

¼–½ teaspoon chili powder (hot or mild)

Salt and ground black pepper

SANDWICH

2 teaspoons canola oil

2 tart apples, peeled, cored and thinly sliced

¼ cup (2 fl oz/60 ml) apple cider or apple juice

1 cup drained sauerkraut

8 slices rye bread

8 slices Swiss cheese

8 oz (240 g) thinly sliced corned beef

For the spread, in a small bowl stir together the mayonnaise, ketchup, onion, pickle, parsley and chili powder; add salt and pepper to taste. (The spread will keep, covered, in the refrigerator for up to 2 days.)

For the sandwiches, in a sauté pan, heat the oil over medium-high heat. Add the apples and cook, stirring, until they start to brown, 3–5 minutes. Add the cider and cook, stirring, until the cider has been absorbed, about 2 minutes more. Remove from the heat and stir in the sauerkraut.

Arrange the bread slices in a single layer on a work surface. Spread a layer of the spread on all 8 slices and place a slice of cheese on top of each. (Be careful not to let the cheese hang over the edges of the bread.) Divide the corned beef and sauerkraut mixture among 4 of the slices and top with the remaining 4 slices of bread, cheese side down. If desired, brush with oil or lightly butter the outside of the sandwiches.

Preheat a two-sided electric indoor grill or ridged grill pan according to the manufacturer's instructions.

If using the two-sided grill, place 2 sandwiches on the grill, close cover, and cook until the bread is toasted and the cheese has melted, about 3 minutes. Repeat with the remaining sandwiches.

If using the grill pan, place 2 sandwiches in the pan and cook until the bread is toasted and the cheese has melted, about 6 minutes, turning carefully once midway through the cooking time. Repeat with the remaining sandwiches.

Serve warm.

Serves 4

Chicken with Lemon and Olives

1 broiler-fryer (roasting) chicken, about 4 lb (1.9 kg)

MARINADE

2 tablespoons extra virgin olive oil

2 tablespoons dry Italian white wine

6 large cloves garlic, crushed

4–6 teaspoons fresh oregano leaves or 2–3 teaspoons dried oregano

Red pepper flakes or small whole red chilies (fresh or dried), to taste

Sprigs of fresh oregano

Zest of 1 lemon, cut into thin strips

12 oil-cured black olives

12 cracked Sicilian green olives

Salt

With poultry shears or a large, sharp knife, cut the chicken into 10 serving pieces.

For the marinade, in a large nonaluminum dish, combine all the marinade ingredients, including red pepper flakes or chilies to taste. Stir well, then add the chicken pieces. Toss to coat evenly, then cover and refrigerate for a few hours or overnight. Remove from refrigerator 1 hour before cooking.

Prepare a fire in a charcoal grill.

Place the chicken pieces, skin side down, on a grill rack over hot coals. Broil or grill until golden around the edges, about

20 minutes. Turn the chicken over and continue to cook until golden brown around the edges on the second side and opaque throughout when cut with a knife, about 20 minutes longer.

Transfer the chicken to a large serving platter and sprinkle with oregano sprigs, lemon zest, olives and red pepper flakes or chilies to taste. Let rest for at least 30 minutes, to allow the flavors to blend. Add salt to taste and serve at room temperature.

Serves 4

Coriander-Crusted Beef Tenderloin

¼ cup (2 fl oz/60 ml) fresh lime juice

2 tablespoons soy sauce

2 tablespoons canola oil

1 jalapeño chili, seeded and very finely chopped

1 teaspoon grated fresh ginger

16 green (spring) onions, trimmed to about 8 inches (20 cm)

1 tablespoon coriander seeds

1½ teaspoons black peppercorns

1½ teaspoons coarse salt

4 beef tenderloin steaks, cut 1–1¼ inches (2.5–3 cm) thick, about 1–1½ lb (500–720 g) total

2 teaspoons Asian (toasted) sesame oil

½ lime

4 teaspoons coarsely chopped cilantro (fresh coriander)

In a shallow, nonaluminum dish, whisk together the lime juice, soy sauce, oil, jalapeño, and ginger. Add the green (spring) onions and turn to coat. Let stand at room temperature for about 1 hour.

In a spice grinder, pulse the coriander seeds and pepper-corns until coarsely cracked (or put them in a plastic bag and crack them with a rolling pin or heavy pot). Transfer to a small dish and mix in the salt. Rub the steaks on both sides with the sesame oil, then coat them with the spice mixture.

Preheat a two-sided electric indoor grill or ridged grill pan according to the manufacturer's instructions.

If using the two-sided grill, arrange the green onions on the grill, close the cover, and cook until they are browned and tender (turning if necessary to make grill marks on both sides), 8–10 minutes. Set aside and keep them warm.

Place the steaks on the grill, close the cover, and cook until done to your liking, 4–5 minutes for medium-rare. Transfer steaks to a cutting board and let stand for 5 minutes.

If using the grill pan, cook the green onions until they are

browned and tender, about 15 minutes, turning them once midway through cooking time. Set aside and keep them warm.

Cook the steaks until done to your liking, 8–10 minutes for medium-rare, turning them once midway through cooking time. Transfer to a cutting board and let stand for 5 minutes.

Cut the steaks into ½-inch (1-cm) thick slices and fan the slices onto 4 plates. Squeeze the lime over the meat and sprinkle with the cilantro. Arrange the green onions next to the steaks and serve immediately.

Serves 4

115

Middle Eastern Chicken Kabobs

1 onion, chopped

4 cloves garlic, chopped

¼ cup (2 fl oz/60 ml) fresh lemon juice

1 tablespoon chopped fresh thyme or 1½ teaspoons dried

1 tablespoon paprika

½ teaspoon cayenne pepper

½ teaspoon ground black pepper

1 cup (8 oz/240 g) natural (plain) yogurt

1 lb (480 g) boneless, skinless chicken breasts, cut into 1-inch (2.5-cm) cubes

Salt and ground black pepper

In a food processor, place the onion, garlic, lemon juice, thyme, paprika, cayenne pepper and black pepper. Pulse until well combined. Add the yogurt and pulse until blended. Pour the marinade into a nonreactive bowl or dish. Add the chicken and turn to coat. Cover and refrigerate for 6–8 hours.

Preheat a two-sided electric indoor grill or ridged grill pan according to the manufacturer's instructions.

Remove chicken pieces from marinade; wipe off any excess.

If using the two-sided grill, thread the chicken pieces onto skewers, leaving a little space between the pieces. Sprinkle with salt and pepper. Place the skewers on the grill, close the cover and cook, in batches if necessary, until the chicken is no longer pink in the center, 2–3 minutes.

If using the grill pan, thread the chicken pieces onto skewers, leaving a little space between the pieces. Sprinkle with salt and pepper. Cook, in batches if necessary, until the chicken is no longer pink in the center, 4–6 minutes, turning once midway through the cooking time. Serve immediately.

Serves 4

Steak with Onion and Cilantro Relish

MARINADE

4 dried Anaheim chilies

4 dried árbol chilies

2 teaspoons cumin seeds

1 clove garlic, very finely chopped

1 fresh jalapeño chili, stemmed, seeded and coarsely chopped

1/2 cup (4 fl oz/120 ml) red wine vinegar

1/2 cup (4 fl oz/120 ml) olive oil

1 1/2 teaspoons salt

1 lb (480 g) trimmed skirt or flank steak

ONION AND CILANTRO RELISH

1 small white onion, very finely chopped

1 fresh serrano chili, stemmed, seeded and finely chopped

1/2 cup (3/4 oz/20 g) coarsely chopped cilantro (fresh coriander)

1 teaspoon salt

Juice of 1 lime

1 tablespoon olive oil

Remove the stems from all the dried chilies, then shake out and discard the seeds. Place the chilies in a small saucepan with water just to cover. Bring to a boil, remove from the heat and let stand for 20 minutes to soften. Drain.

In a small, dry frying pan over medium heat, toast the cumin seeds until lightly browned and fragrant, 2–3 minutes. In a blender, combine the softened chilies, cumin seeds, garlic, jalapeño chili and red wine vinegar. Purée until thick and smooth, 1–2 minutes. Add the olive oil and salt and blend again until well mixed.

Place the steak in a shallow nonaluminum dish and pour the marinade over it. Let marinate at room temperature for 1 hour.

Prepare a fire in a charcoal grill.

Just before placing the steak on the grill, make the relish: In a small bowl, stir together the onion, serrano chili, cilantro, salt, lime juice and oil. Set aside until ready to serve.

When the fire is hot, place the steak on the grill rack about 3 inches (7.5 cm) from the coals. Grill, turning once, until seared on the outside but still pink in the center, 1–2 minutes per side.

To serve, slice the steak across the grain and on the diagonal. Arrange the slices on a platter and serve with the relish.

Serves 4

Cornish Hens with Grilled Vegetables

2 Cornish hens (spatchcocks),
3–4 lb (1.4–1.9 kg) total weight,
cut in halves

MARINADE

⅓ cup (2½ fl oz/75 ml) extra
virgin olive oil

½ cup (4 fl oz/120 ml) balsamic
vinegar

1 tablespoon chopped garlic

3 tablespoons chopped golden
(French) shallots

4 teaspoons fresh rosemary
or 2 teaspoons dried rosemary

15 fresh sage leaves or
1 teaspoon ground dried sage

2 bay leaves

Ground black pepper

VEGETABLES

1 small head broccoli

1 small head cauliflower

1 zucchini (courgette)

1 whole head garlic

2 yellow onions, cut in halves

1 cup (8 fl oz/240 ml) water,
or as needed

Meat and Poultry

Prepare a fire in a charcoal grill or preheat a gas grill to medium-high heat.

For the marinade, in a shallow nonaluminum dish, combine all the marinade ingredients, including pepper to taste. Place hens in marinade, turning to coat evenly. Cover and refrigerate overnight, turning once.

To prepare the vegetables, cut the broccoli and cauliflower lengthwise into small florets. Cut the zucchini in halves lengthwise and then in halves crosswise. Remove some outside layers of papery skin from the head of garlic and cut off the top one-fourth of the head, exposing the cloves.

Remove hens from marinade, reserving the marinade, and place the hen halves on the grill rack, skin-side down. Grill for 20 minutes, then turn and baste with the reserved marinade.

Continue to grill until the hens are a deep brown and cooked through when cut with a knife, about 20 minutes longer.

During the last 20 minutes of cooking, arrange the vegetables, including the onions, on the grill rack. Cook until tender and browned in places, 8–15 minutes.

Check the vegetables frequently; when done to your liking, remove from grill and keep warm.

Place a hen half on each of 4 serving plates and serve the vegetables alongside.

Serves 4

122

Pork Satay

MARINADE AND PORK

2 tablespoons brown sugar

1½ teaspoons ground coriander

1 teaspoon ground cumin

½ teaspoon ground turmeric

1 tablespoon fresh lime juice

1½ teaspoons Thai or Vietnamese fish sauce

2 tablespoons coconut cream

1½ lb (720 g) pork butt or tenderloin, cut into ¾-inch (2-cm) cubes

SATAY SAUCE

1 oz (30 g) tamarind pulp, coarsely chopped

½ cup (4 fl oz/120 ml) boiling water

1 tablespoon peanut or corn oil

2 tablespoons red curry paste

1 tablespoon sweet paprika

1 cup (8 fl oz/240 ml) coconut milk

¾ cup (1½ oz/45 g) ground dry-roasted peanuts or 6 table-spoons (3 oz/90 g) chunky peanut butter

2 tablespoons palm sugar or brown sugar

1 tablespoon Thai or Vietnamese fish sauce

½ teaspoon salt

For the marinade, in a bowl, combine brown sugar, coriander, cumin, turmeric, lime juice, fish sauce and coconut cream. Add the pork and mix thoroughly to coat. Cover and let marinate for 2 hours at room temperature.

Soak 18 bamboo skewers in cold water for at least 30 minutes.

For the sauce, in a small bowl, soak the tamarind pulp in the boiling water for 15 minutes. Mash with the back of a fork to help dissolve the pulp. Pour through a fine-mesh sieve into another small bowl, pressing against the pulp to extract as much liquid as possible. Discard the pulp; set the liquid aside.

Place a wok or saucepan over medium heat. When hot, add the oil, curry paste and paprika. Reduce heat to low and cook, stirring, for 1 minute. Add the coconut milk and stir constantly over low heat until a red-stained oil shows through the paste, about 3 minutes. Add the peanuts or peanut butter and palm sugar or brown sugar and simmer, stirring occasionally, for about 5 minutes.

Stir in the tamarind liquid, fish sauce and salt and cook for 1 minute longer. If the sauce is too thick, thin it with a little water. Remove from the heat and keep warm.

Prepare a fire in a charcoal grill or preheat a gas grill to medium–high heat. Thread 4 or 5 pieces of pork onto each skewer. The pieces should touch, but do not press them together. Discard the marinade. Place skewers on grill rack and cook until grill marks show on the underside, about 2 minutes. Turn skewers and continue grilling until pork is browned on all sides and firm to the touch, 1–2 minutes longer.

To serve, arrange the skewers on a platter. Pour the sauce into a shallow serving bowl and serve alongside.

Serves 6

Glazed Ham Steaks with Mango

Oil or melted butter, for brushing

4 thick ham steaks

1½ tablespoons brown sugar

2 tablespoons butter

Salt and ground black pepper, to taste

2 fresh medium-sized mangoes

Prepare a fire in a charcoal grill or preheat a gas grill to medium heat.

Cut 4 pieces of aluminum foil, each 12 inches (30 cm) square. Brush with oil or melted butter. Place a ham steak on each.

Make a paste with the brown sugar, butter, salt and pepper and spread thickly over one side of each steak. Peel and thickly slice the mangoes and spread slices evenly over each steak, using half a mango to each. Wrap the foil around the parcels and fold the edges together to seal.

Place the parcels on the grill rack and cook over medium heat for about 6 minutes, or place on a baking tray and cook in a hot oven for 15 minutes.

Serves 4

Squab with Garlic and Ginger

4 squab, Cornish hens or poussins, about 1 lb (480 g) each

3 tablespoons vegetable oil

1 tablespoon finely grated ginger

2 large garlic cloves, mashed

1½ teaspoons salt

1½ teaspoons ground black pepper

1 medium onion, thinly sliced

1 small cucumber, thinly sliced

1 medium carrot, thinly sliced

2 teaspoons sugar

1½ tablespoons white wine vinegar

Rinse and thoroughly dry the squab, then cut in halves down the backbone and breastbone and press each half out flat. Rub with a little of the oil. Mix the ginger, garlic, ¾ teaspoon of the salt and the pepper together and rub evenly over the chicken. Set aside for 1 hour.

Prepare a fire in a charcoal grill or preheat a gas grill to medium heat.

Place the squab on the grill rack and cook, brushing occasionally with the remaining oil and turning several times, until the surface is golden brown and the meat feels firm when pressed, 15–20 minutes.

Place the vegetables in a dish. Mix the remaining salt with the sugar and vinegar and pour over the vegetables. Knead with your fingers for a few minutes until softened. Arrange the squab on warmed plates and serve with the marinated vegetables.

NOTE The vegetables can be marinated up to 2 days in advance and stored in a covered container in the refrigerator. Marinate the squab, wrapped in plastic film and refrigerated, up to 1 day in advance.

Serves 4

Mesquite-Smoked Cornish Hens

2 cups mesquite wood chips,
for smoking

4 Cornish hens or poussins

3 tablespoons (1 1/2 oz /45 g)
butter, softened, plus extra
for brushing

2 medium cloves garlic, mashed

1/2 teaspoon salt

1/2 teaspoon ground black pepper

1/4 teaspoon cayenne pepper
(optional)

Soak the mesquite in cold water overnight, or for at least several hours, then drain well.

Cut the hens in halves down the backbone and breastbone. Rinse and dry well. Mix the butter, garlic, salt, pepper and cayenne to a paste and spread over hens.

Prepare a fire in a charcoal grill. Add the wood chips to the grill and place hens, skin-side down, on the rack over the coals.

Cover and cook for 15 minutes, then turn and cook the other side until done, 15–20 minutes longer, brushing with a little extra butter from time to time to keep the hens moist.

To test if done, insert a fine skewer into the thickest part of the meat; the juices should run clear.

Serves 4

Grilled Duck Breasts with Fig Sauce

2 plump ducks, about 2 lb
(1.9 kg) each

1 small onion

1 small carrot

1 bay leaf

2 peppercorns

4 cups (960 ml) water

6 oz (180 g) dried figs

1 cup (8 fl oz/240 ml) dry sherry

1 small cinnamon stick

1 whole clove

1 cup (8 fl oz/240 ml) orange
juice

Salt and ground black pepper

2 tablespoons (1 oz/30 g)
unsalted butter, melted

Using a sharp knife, remove the breasts from the ducks. Place the necks, wings and backbones of the ducks in a saucepan to make a stock. Wrap and chill the duck breasts. Freeze the remainder of the ducks for another use.

Add the onion, carrot, bay leaf, peppercorns and water to the stockpot. Bring to a boil, reduce the heat and simmer for 1 hour, skimming surface occasionally.

Meanwhile, in a saucepan, soak the figs in the sherry with the cinnamon stick and clove. Strain the duck stock into a smaller pan and boil to reduce to 1 cup (8 fl oz/250 ml). Remove and discard the spices from the figs

and add the stock. Simmer gently until the figs are very tender, then purée the figs and their cooking liquid in a blender or food processor. Return the purée to the saucepan and add the orange juice and salt and pepper to taste. Boil to make a very thick sauce.

Prepare a fire in a charcoal grill or preheat a gas grill to medium-high heat.

Season the duck breasts with salt and pepper. Brush with melted butter and cook on the grill rack for about 15 minutes, until cooked through. Turn several times during cooking to brown the surface evenly. Test if done by piercing with a fine skewer: if the juices run clear, the breasts are done.

The breasts can also be cooked in a medium oven. Melt the butter in a hot oven dish on the stovetop, add the breasts and brown them, turning once. Place dish in a preheated moderate oven and cook for 25 minutes, or until done to your liking.

Serve on warmed plates, coated with the sauce. Accompany with steamed or grilled vegetables.

NOTE The sauce can be made in advance and refrigerated until needed.

Serves 4

Chicken Burger with Onion Relish

ONION RELISH

¼ cup (2 fl oz/60 ml) olive oil

3 Spanish onions, thinly sliced

1 teaspoon sugar

2 tablespoons balsamic vinegar

BURGERS

½ cup (4 fl oz/125 ml) good-quality extra virgin olive oil

1 eggplant (aubergine), very finely sliced crosswise

4 boneless, skinless chicken breasts, seasoned with salt and cayenne pepper

Lettuce

4 sandwich rolls

For the onion relish, heat the olive oil in a heavy-based pan. Add the onions and cook gently, stirring occasionally, until soft. Add the sugar and vinegar and simmer for 10 minutes. The relish will keep for 3 days, covered, in the refrigerator. Return to room temperature or reheat before use.

For the burgers, heat 3 tablespoons of the oil in a heavy-based pan. Add the eggplant slices and cook until golden. Set aside on paper towels to drain.

Add 3 tablespoons oil to the pan and cook chicken breasts slowly until golden and tender.

Brush the bread rolls with some of the olive oil. Place a lettuce leaf on the base of each roll, then top with chicken, eggplant and onion relish. Replace roll top and serve immediately.

Serves 4

Marinated Barbecued Leg of Lamb

1 leg of lamb, about 6 lb (2.9 kg), boned and trimmed of excess fat

4–6 cloves garlic, slivered

3 tablespoons vegetable oil or melted butter

Cracked black pepper

MARINADE

2 tablespoons red wine vinegar

2 cups (16 fl oz/480 ml) dry white or red wine

1 teaspoon black peppercorns

4 bay leaves

1 teaspoon juniper berries

2 sprigs parsley

1 medium onion, chopped

1 small carrot, chopped

1 teaspoon salt

Pierce the lamb in several places with the point of a knife and insert the garlic slivers evenly over the whole leg. Mix all the marinade ingredients in a large nonaluminum dish. Add lamb, turn to coat, cover with plastic wrap and let marinate in the refrigerator or in a cool place for 24 hours, turning several times.

Drain well, discarding marinade. Pat the surface of the lamb with paper towels to dry it. Rub with oil or melted butter, then season with pepper.

Prepare a fire in a charcoal grill or preheat a gas grill to medium heat. Brush the grill rack with oil and cook the lamb over medium heat until the surface is well crisped and the meat is just cooked through, 45–60 minutes. Turn several times during cooking, basting each time with extra oil or butter.

Remove from the heat and allow to rest in a warm place for 5–6 minutes. Slice and serve with salads or baked potatoes.

Serves 6

Barbecued Meat Kabobs

Salt and ground black pepper

2 tablespoons light soy sauce

2 teaspoons sugar

1 tablespoon dry sherry or brandy

12 oz (360 g) lean tender beef, such as tenderloin, fillet or rump, cut into 1-inch (2.5-cm) cubes

6 baby lamb cutlets, frenched (see glossary)

1 clove garlic, mashed

3 sheep kidneys

3 slices (rashers) fat bacon

1 large boneless, skinless chicken breast, cut crosswise into 6 pieces

2 tablespoons olive oil

Lemon–pepper seasoning

3 spicy sausages, such as honeywurst or Italian, cut in halves crosswise

6 small bay leaves

6 button mushrooms

6 large cherry tomatoes

2 tablespoons or oil

In a shallow bowl, mix salt, pepper, soy sauce, sugar and sherry or brandy. Add beef and marinate for 20 minutes.

Rub cutlets with garlic and set aside. Cut the kidneys in halves, remove the fat core and wrap a half slice of bacon around each.

Rub the chicken with oil, then sprinkle with lemon pepper.

Thread each meat alternately onto oiled metal skewers, adding a bay leaf, mushroom and tomato to each. Brush with oil and cook on a grill rack, turning frequently, until done to your liking.

Serves 6

Beef Kabobs with Mint Chutney

1 lb (480 g) lean tender beef (tenderloin, fillet or rump)

1 small onion, grated

1–2 cloves garlic, mashed

½-inch (1-cm) piece fresh ginger, grated

2 tablespoons vegetable oil

1 tablespoon dark soy sauce

¼ teaspoon salt

½ teaspoon black pepper

4–6 large green (spring) onions

Extra oil or melted butter

MINTED COCONUT CHUTNEY

1 cup (1½ oz/45 g) loosely packed fresh mint leaves

1 medium onion

½ cup (1 oz/30 g) grated dried (desiccated) coconut

¼ teaspoon black mustard seeds (optional)

¼ cup (2 fl oz/60 ml) white vinegar

2–3 tablespoons sugar

Salt to taste

Trim the meat and cut into 1-inch (2.5-cm) cubes. Place in a dish. Combine the onion, garlic, ginger, oil, soy sauce, salt and pepper and mix well. Brush meat with the mixture. Cover the meat with plastic wrap and set aside for 40 minutes.

Prepare a fire in a charcoal grill or preheat a gas grill to medium-high heat.

Cut green onions into 1¼-inch (3-cm) lengths. Thread the meat and onions alternately onto oiled metal skewers. Brush with some of the extra oil or butter and grill, turning frequently, until done to your liking.

Meanwhile, make the chutney. In a food processor, chop the mint leaves finely; remove. Process onion to a smooth paste, add the remaining ingredients and the mint, and process until well mixed.

Serve kabobs on a bed of rice with the chutney on the side.

Serves 6

NOTE The kabobs can be marinated and threaded onto bamboo skewers several hours in advance, or the night before. Wrap tightly or cover with plastic wrap and refrigerate. The chutney can be made up to 3 days in advance.

Beef Rolls with Blue Cheese Sauce

8 thin beef or veal steaks, about
1¼ lb (600 g)

8 spears fresh asparagus

8 thin slices cooked ham

Salt and pepper

1 tablespoon olive oil

BLUE CHEESE SAUCE

2 tablespoons butter

1½ tablespoons all-purpose
(plain) flour

¼ cup (2 fl oz/60 ml) white wine

1 cup (8 fl oz/240 ml) milk

¼ cup (1 oz/30 g) grated
Cheddar cheese

¾ cup (3 oz/90 g) blue vein
cheese

Prepare a fire in a charcoal grill or preheat a gas grill to medium-high heat.

Place steaks on a work surface, cover with plastic wrap, and gently pound with a meat mallet. Trim asparagus spears to even lengths and parboil in lightly salted water for 3 minutes. Drain, cool under cold running water, and drain again.

Place a slice of ham and spear of asparagus on each steak. Season with salt and pepper to taste. Roll up, secure with tooth-picks, and brush with oil. Grill, turning frequently, until the meat is done to your liking.

Meanwhile, for the cheese sauce, melt the butter in a small pan, add the flour and cook briefly, then stir in the wine and milk. Boil, stirring continuously, until thickened.

Add the cheeses and salt and pepper to taste and cook until the cheeses melt and the sauce is creamy. Arrange rolls on a platter and pour on the sauce or serve separately.

Serves 4

Sell your books at
sellbackyourBook.com!
Go to sellbackyourBook.com
and get an instant price
quote. We even pay the
shipping - see what your old
books are worth today!

Inspected By: Marisol_Garcia

00003639

8796

Marinated Honeyed Pork Spare Ribs

1 cup (8 fl oz/240 ml) plum sauce

1 cup (8 fl oz/240 ml) barbecue sauce

1 cup (8 fl oz/240 ml) sweet sherry

1 cup (8 fl oz/240 ml) olive or safflower oil

½ cup (4 fl oz/120 ml) honey

1 teaspoon dried cumin

1 teaspoon dried cardamom

1 teaspoon dried turmeric

4 lb (1.9 kg) pork spare ribs

Combine all ingredients, except ribs, in a large shallow dish. Add ribs and turn to coat with the marinade. Cover and marinate in refrigerator overnight, brushing frequently with marinade.

Prepare a fire in a charcoal grill or preheat a gas grill to medium-high heat.

Barbecue ribs for about 40 minutes, basting frequently with marinade and turning during cooking.

Serves 8

Racks of Lamb with Oriental Crust

1 medium onion

2 cloves garlic

½-inch (1-cm) piece fresh ginger, roughly chopped

2 slices white bread, crusts removed

Salt and pepper

1 teaspoon lemongrass powder

2 tablespoons ground coriander

1 tablespoon oil

2 tablespoons light soy sauce

2 teaspoons dry sherry

4 racks of lamb, each containing 3–4 cutlets

Combine onion, garlic, ginger and bread in a food processor and pulse until chopped. Add the lemongrass, coriander, oil, soy sauce and sherry and mix to a smooth paste. Place the lamb racks in a dish, spread with the seasoning and set aside to marinate for 30 minutes.

Prepare a fire in a charcoal grill or preheat a gas grill to medium-high heat.

Place the lamb on the grill rack and cook for about 35 minutes, or until done to your liking, turning once.

NOTE Crust can be prepared at least 1 day in advance. Cover with plastic wrap and refrigerate until needed.

Serves 4

Chicken Thighs with Mole Sauce

SAUCE

2 tablespoons vegetable oil

½ cup (2 oz/60 g) sliced (flaked) almonds

1 onion, chopped

2 cloves garlic, chopped

½ teaspoon salt

3 tablespoons chili powder

¼ teaspoon ground cinnamon

¼ teaspoon ground coriander

⅛ teaspoon ground cloves

1 can (8 fl oz/240 ml) tomato sauce

¾ cup (6 fl oz/180 ml) chicken stock

½ small corn tortilla, torn into pieces .

¼ cup (1½ oz/45 g) raisins

1 oz (30 g) bittersweet (not semisweet) chocolate, coarsely chopped

CHICKEN

6 bone-in chicken thighs, trimmed of excess fat

Salt and ground black pepper

For the sauce, in a medium frying pan heat 1 tablespoon of the oil over medium–high heat. Add almonds and cook, stirring, until golden and toasted, about 3 minutes; transfer to a blender or food processor and let cool.

Add the onion and remaining oil to the skillet; reduce the heat to medium and cook, stirring, until onion is softened, about 5 minutes.

In a small bowl, mash the garlic and salt to make a paste. Add the paste to the onion, along with the chili powder, cinnamon, coriander and cloves; cook until fragrant, about 2 minutes more.

Add the onion mixture to the almonds in the blender or food processor. Add the tomato sauce, chicken stock and tortilla pieces; blend until smooth. Return the mixture to the frying pan and add the raisins and chocolate; stir over medium heat until the chocolate is melted.

Preheat a large two-sided electric indoor grill or ridged grill pan according to the manufacturer's instructions.

Season both sides of the chicken with salt and pepper.

If using the two-sided grill, place the chicken on the grill, close the cover, and cook until the chicken is no longer pink next to the bone, 8–10 minutes.

If using the grill pan, cook until chicken is no longer pink next to the bone, 15–20 minutes, turning once midway through the cooking time.

Rewarm the sauce and spoon over the chicken.

Serves 3

NOTE Mole (MO-lay) means "concoction," and there are limitless variations on this classic rich Mexican sauce, which is usually slow-simmered. This fast version is great served with rice and a salad of greens, red onion and sliced oranges.

Sirloin Steak in Coffee Marinade

MARINADE

1/3 cup (2½ fl oz/75 ml) olive oil

1/3 cup (2½ fl oz/75 ml) cider vinegar

1/4 cup (1 oz/30 g) chopped golden (French) shallots

1½ tablespoons finely ground coffee

1 tablespoon ground black pepper

1 teaspoon Dijon mustard

1 teaspoon salt

STEAK

1½ lb (720 g) boneless sirloin steak, trimmed of excess fat and cut into 4 equal pieces

For the marinade, in a shallow, nonaluminum dish just large enough to hold the steak, whisk together the oil, vinegar, shallots, coffee, pepper, mustard and salt.

Add the steak, turning to coat it well. Cover tightly with plastic wrap and refrigerate for at least 6 hours or as long as overnight.

Preheat a two-sided electric indoor grill or ridged grill pan according to the manufacturer's instructions.

Remove the steak from the marinade, shaking off the excess.

If using the two-sided grill, place the steak on the grill, close the cover, and cook until done to your liking, 4–5 minutes for medium rare.

If using the grill pan, cook the steak until done to your liking, 8–10 minutes for medium rare, turning once midway through the cooking time.

Transfer the steak to a platter and let stand for 5 minutes before serving.

Serves 4

Blue Cheese Burgers with Onions

1 tablespoon olive oil

2 onions, thinly sliced

1 teaspoon sugar

Salt and ground black pepper

2 oz (60 g) blue cheese

1 1/4 lb (600 g) ground (minced) sirloin

4 hamburger buns

2 cups (4 oz / 120 g) fresh watercress sprigs

In a large frying pan, heat the oil over medium-low heat. Add the onions and sugar and cook, stirring occasionally, until golden, 10–20 minutes. Add salt and pepper to taste. Set aside.

Cut the cheese into four squares about 1 1/4 x 1 1/4 x 1 1/4 inches (3 x 3 x 3 cm) each. Surround each square of cheese with one quarter of the ground beef and form the meat around the cheese into a patty. Add salt and pepper to taste.

Preheat a ridged grill pan according to the manufacturer's instructions.

Cook the burgers until they are well browned and the cheese has melted, 8–10 minutes for medium, turning them once midway through the cooking time. (Flip them carefully, so the melted cheese does not leak from the center. Do not press on the burgers during cooking.)

To serve, toast the hamburger buns, then arrange the watercress, burgers and caramelized onions on the toasted buns.

Serves 4

Blackened Chicken with Spicy Sauce

SPICY SAUCE

1/3 cup (2 1/2 fl oz/75 ml) tomato sauce (purée)

1 tomato, finely chopped

1 tablespoon lime juice, plus
1 teaspoon extra

1 tablespoon chili sauce, plus
1 teaspoon extra

1/4 teaspoon hot-pepper sauce, such as Tabasco

1/2 teaspoon salt

2 teaspoons chopped fresh dill

Ground black pepper to taste

CHICKEN

6 boneless, skinless chicken breast halves

1 tablespoon paprika, plus
1 teaspoon extra

2 teaspoons black pepper

1/2 teaspoon cayenne pepper, or to taste

2 teaspoons garlic powder

2 teaspoons onion powder

1 teaspoon salt

1 teaspoon dried thyme

1/2 cup (4 oz/125 g) butter, melted

For the sauce, combine all the ingredients in a bowl; mix well. Stand for at least 1 hour.

Using a meat mallet, lightly pound the chicken until thinner and of an even thickness.

Combine paprika, black pepper, cayenne pepper, garlic and onion powders, salt and thyme in a screw-top jar; shake well.

Prepare a fire in a charcoal grill or preheat a gas grill to high heat, or preheat a ridged grill pan to high heat according to the manufacturer's instructions.

Dip the chicken into the melted butter and sprinkle the spice mixture on both sides. Cook the chicken for about 2 minutes on each side, or until a black crust forms and the chicken is cooked through. (This cooking process will create a lot of smoke and is best done outdoors. Have a strong exhaust fan operating if cooking indoors.)

Serve the chicken with the sauce and some extra melted butter, if desired.

NOTE The spice mix can be made several weeks ahead. Store in an airtight jar at room temperature. The sauce can be made a day ahead.

Serves 6

Chicken with Vegetables and Aïoli

½ cup (4 fl oz/120 ml) olive oil

¼ cup (2 fl oz/60 ml) lemon juice

2 cloves garlic, crushed

4 green (spring) onions, chopped

1 tablespoon chopped fresh thyme

1 broiler-fryer (roasting) chicken, about 2 lb (1.9 kg), cut into serving pieces

AÏOLI

2 egg yolks

¼ teaspoon salt

2 cloves garlic, crushed

⅔ cup (5 fl oz/150 ml) olive oil

⅓ cup (2½ fl oz/75 ml) olive oil

1 tablespoon lemon juice

VEGETABLES

4 small Asian (slender) eggplants (aubergines)

2 green zucchini (courgettes)

2 yellow squash zucchini (courgettes)

2 red bell peppers (capsicums)

4 medium red-skinned potatoes

Coarse salt

Ground black pepper

2 large florets broccoli

Serves 4–6

Prepare a fire in a covered grill.

Combine the oil, lemon juice, garlic, green onions and thyme and brush the chicken pieces with some of this mixture. Cook on a covered grill over very low heat for about 45 minutes, or until almost done, turning once during cooking. Or, bake chicken at 375°F (190°C) for about 45 minutes, or until almost done. Finish the chicken on a charcoal or gas grill to brown it and enhance its flavor.

For the aïoli, blend or process the egg yolks, salt and garlic until smooth. Gradually add the oils in a thin stream with the motor running until the mixture is thick. Transfer to a bowl and stir in the lemon juice.

Thinly slice the eggplants (aubergines) and the zucchini (courgettes) lengthways. Cut the bell peppers (capsicums) into thick strips; thinly slice the potatoes. Brush the vegetables with some of the oil mixture.

About 15 minutes before the chicken is done, add the vegetables to the grill and and barbecue beside the chicken until well browned and tender, about 10 minutes. Drizzle with the remaining oil mixture and serve with salt, pepper and aïoli.

Stuffed Chicken Thighs

3 oz (90 g) chopped prosciutto

½ cup (2 oz/60 g) shredded Fontina cheese

2 teaspoons chopped fresh sage, plus 6 sage leaves

¼ cup (1 oz/30 g) unseasoned dry breadcrumbs

¼ cup (1 oz/30 g) freshly grated Parmesan cheese

8 boneless, skinless chicken thighs

1 tablespoon olive oil

In a bowl, stir together the prosciutto, Fontina cheese, and chopped sage. In another bowl, combine the breadcrumbs and Parmesan.

Open the chicken thighs flat and place between two sheets of plastic wrap; pound gently with a meat mallet to flatten.

Preheat a two-sided electric indoor grill.

Place some of the prosciutto mixture over one half of each thigh and fold the other half firmly on top. Brush the chicken with olive oil, then dip in the breadcrumb mixture.

Place the chicken on the grill, setting a sage leaf on top of each piece. Close the cover and cook, in batches as necessary, until the chicken is no longer pink in the center, about 5 minutes. Serve immediately.

Serves 4

NOTE Boneless chicken thighs are a natural for stuffing, but flattening them before grilling helps them cook more quickly and evenly.

Roast Beef Hash Patties

1 cup (4 oz/120 g) unseasoned dry breadcrumbs

4 tablespoons (2 oz/60 g) butter, melted

2 cups (16 oz/480 g) finely diced leftover cooked roast beef or steak

2 cups (16 oz/480 g) finely diced cooked potatoes

1 small onion, finely chopped

1/4 cup (2 fl oz/60 ml) cream or milk

1/2 teaspoon salt

1/4 teaspoon ground black pepper

In a small bowl, stir together the breadcrumbs and butter until well combined; spread out on a small plate.

In another bowl, combine the beef, potatoes, onion, cream or milk, salt and pepper. Mash the mixture with a fork until it is combined and holds together well. Shape into 4 equal patties.

Preheat a two-sided electric indoor grill or ridged grill pan according to the manufacturer's instructions.

Press both sides of each patty into the breadcrumbs.

If using the two-sided grill, place the patties on the grill, close the cover, and cook until nicely browned, about 3 minutes.

If using the grill pan, cook until the patties are nicely browned, about 6 minutes, turning once midway through cooking time.

Serve at once.

Serves 4

157

Deluxe Sirloin Burgers

1½ tablespoons fresh lemon juice

¼ cup (2 fl oz/60 ml) extra virgin olive oil

4 thick slices tomato

4 thick slices red (Spanish) onion

1 teaspoon salt, plus extra as needed

½ teaspoon ground black pepper, plus extra as needed

1 lb (480 g) ground (minced) sirloin

⅓ cup (2½ fl oz/75 ml) hot-pepper sauce, such as Tabasco

2 tablespoons ice water

4 large rolls or hamburger buns

Shredded iceberg lettuce, to serve

In a shallow, nonaluminum dish, combine the lemon juice and 3 tablespoons of the olive oil. Add the tomato and onion slices and turn to coat. Add salt and pepper and set aside.

Preheat a two-sided electric indoor grill or ridged grill pan according to the manufacturer's instructions.

In a bowl, combine the sirloin, salt, pepper, hot-pepper sauce and ice water. Mix well. Wet your hands, then gently form the mixture into four 1-inch (2.5 cm) thick patties.

If using the two-sided grill, place the burgers on the grill, close the cover and cook until done to your liking, 4–7 minutes for medium.

If using the grill pan, cook the burgers until done to your liking, 8–14 minutes for medium, turning once midway through the cooking time.

Toast the buns, then brush the cut sides with the remaining olive oil. Place each burger on the bottom half of a bun and top with a slice of tomato and onion and one-fourth of the lettuce.

Serves 4

Honey-Glazed Drumsticks

¼ cup (2 fl oz/60 ml) honey

2 tablespoons soy sauce

1 tablespoon cider vinegar

1 tablespoon molasses (optional)

8 chicken drumsticks, about 2¼ lb (1 kg) total

In a small saucepan, combine the honey, soy sauce, vinegar and molasses, if using. Cook over medium–low heat for about 5 minutes, or until bubbly, stirring occasionally. (Watch mixture closely, as it will foam.)

Meanwhile, prepare a fire in a charcoal grill or preheat a gas grill to medium-high heat. If desired, remove skin from chicken. Rinse chicken; pat dry. Place on the grill rack and grill for about 15 minutes, or until chicken is light brown. Turn and cook for 10–15 minutes more, or until chicken is tender and no pink remains. Brush chicken with the glaze during the last

5–10 minutes of broiling. Before serving, spoon any remaining glaze over drumsticks.

Serves 4

Steak with Grilled Onion Guacamole

STEAK

1/3 cup (2 1/2 fl oz/75 ml) fresh lime juice

3 tablespoons olive oil

2 tablespoons tequila

2 tablespoons orange liqueur, such as triple sec, Cointreau or Grand Marnier

2 teaspoons sugar

1 lb (480 g) top round steak, cut 1 inch (2.5 cm) thick

Salt and ground black pepper

GUACAMOLE

1 large red onion, cut into 1/2-inch (1-cm) thick slices

2 tablespoons extra virgin olive oil

2 ripe avocados, pitted and peeled

1 clove garlic, finely chopped

1 jalapeño chili, seeded and finely chopped

4 teaspoons fresh lime juice

1 tablespoon chopped cilantro (fresh coriander)

1/2 teaspoon salt, plus extra as needed

In a shallow, nonaluminum dish, whisk together the lime juice, oil, tequila, liqueur and sugar. Add the steak and turn to coat. Cover and refrigerate for 4 hours, turning the steak once or twice.

Preheat a two-sided electric indoor grill or ridged grill pan according to the manufacturer's instructions. Remove the steak from the marinade, shaking off the excess. Season generously on both sides with salt and pepper.

If using the two-sided grill, coat onions with oil, arrange on the grill, close cover and cook until onions are tender and charred, about 5 minutes. Let cool.

Place steak on grill, close cover, and cook until done to your liking, 3–4 minutes for medium-rare. Transfer to a cutting board and let stand for 5 minutes.

If using the grill pan, coat onions with oil, then grill until tender and charred, 6–8 minutes, turning once midway through the cooking time. Let cool.

Then cook the steak until done to your liking, 6–8 minutes for medium-rare, turning once midway through the cooking time. Transfer to a cutting board and let stand for 5 minutes.

While the steak is cooking, prepare the guacamole. Coarsely

chop the grilled onions. In a mixing bowl, coarsely mash the avocados with a fork. Fold in the onions, garlic, jalapeño, lime juice, cilantro and salt. Taste and add more salt if needed.

To serve, thinly slice the meat across the grain, top with the guacamole and serve immediately.

Serves 4

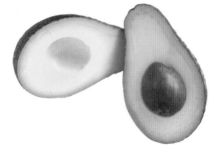

Citrus-Marinated Chicken Breast

MARINADE

½ cup (4 fl oz/125 ml) fresh
orange juice

1 tablespoon fresh lime juice

½ dried chipotle chili, stemmed
and seeded

½ cup (4 fl oz/125 ml) Smooth
Red Salsa (page 69) or tomato
purée

2 tablespoons olive oil

1 teaspoon salt

CHICKEN

4 boneless, skinless chicken breast
halves, about 1 lb (480 g) total

Fresh orange slices and cilantro
sprigs, for garnish (optional)

For the marinade, in a small
saucepan, combine the orange
juice, lime juice and chili and
bring the mixture to a boil.
Reduce the heat to maintain a
simmer and cook, uncovered,
until the chili is softened, about
5 minutes. Remove from the
heat and let cool completely.

Transfer the mixture to a
blender and add the salsa, oil
and salt. Purée until smooth.

For the chicken, place the
chicken breasts between 2 sheets
of plastic wrap; pound with the
flat side of a meat mallet until
evenly thick. Place the chicken
in a shallow, nonaluminum dish

and add the marinade, turning
the chicken to coat it. Cover and
refrigerate for 2–4 hours.

Preheat a two-sided electric
indoor grill or ridged grill pan
according to the manufacturer's
instructions.

Remove the chicken from the
marinade, shaking off the excess.

If using the two-sided grill,
place the chicken on the grill,
close the cover and cook until
the chicken is no longer pink
in the center, 4–5 minutes.

If using the grill pan, cook the
chicken until it is no longer pink
in the center, 8–10 minutes,

turning once midway through the cooking time.

Transfer the chicken to a platter and garnish with orange slices and cilantro, if desired.

Serves 4

Pork Chops with Chutney Glaze

4 large pork chops

1/2 teaspoon salt

1/3 teaspoon ground black pepper

3 tablespoons bottled fruit chutney

1 teaspoon vindaloo paste or other hot curry sauce

2–3 tablespoons vegetable oil

Hot cooked couscous, to serve

1 cucumber, thinly sliced lengthwise, to serve (optional)

Prepare a fire in a charcoal grill or preheat a gas grill to medium–high heat.

Trim excess fat from the chops and season with salt and pepper. Make a paste with the chutney and vindaloo or curry paste and brush over both sides of each chop. Set the remainder aside.

Place chops on grill rack and cook, turning frequently and brushing with oil. When chops are almost done, spread the remaining chutney thickly over one side and continue to cook on the other side until done.

Serve with couscous and cucumber slices, if liked.

Serves 4

NOTE Chutney is a tangy Indian relish eaten in small quantities to add piquancy to a meal. In India, a chutney is almost always a mixture of ground raw ingredients, such as ginger, chili, garlic, onion, herbs, sour fruits and coconut. It is made and served fresh. The sweet, bottled chutney known in the West is very different. Although of Indian inspiration, this product is always a cooked mixture of fruit (usually mango, apples, raisins and/or tomato), sugar, vinegar and spices.

Grilled Beef Tacos

GARNISHES

1/4 head iceberg lettuce, shredded

Diced flesh of 2 avocados, mixed with 2 tablespoons lime juice

2 tomatoes, seeded and diced

4 green (spring) onions, sliced

2 tablespoons coarsely chopped cilantro (fresh coriander)

1/2 cup (4 fl oz/120 ml) purchased tomato salsa

BEEF

8 large corn tortillas

1 lb (480 g) skirt or flank steak

Salt and ground black pepper

2 cloves garlic, minced

1 tablespoon olive oil

1 tablespoon fresh lime juice

Prepare all the garnishes, place in serving bowls, and set aside.

Preheat an oven to 300°F (150°C). Preheat a large two-sided electric indoor grill or ridged grill pan according to the manufacturer's instructions.

Directly on top of electric or gas stove burners, lightly toast both sides of the tortillas. Wrap in foil and keep warm in the oven.

Season both sides of steak with salt and pepper. Rub both sides with the minced garlic, then with the olive oil, and drizzle both sides with the lime juice.

If using the two-sided grill, place steak on the grill, close the cover and cook until done to your liking, 4–5 minutes for medium-rare.

If using the grill pan, cook the steak until done to your liking, 8 minutes for medium-rare, turning once midway through the cooking time.

Transfer steak to a cutting board and let stand for 5 minutes. Cut across the grain into 1/4-inch (5-mm) thick slices. Serve with warmed tortillas and garnishes, letting each diner assemble his or her own tacos.

Serves 4

Chicken with Walnut–Sage Pesto

PESTO

1½ cups (6 oz/185 g) walnuts

½ cup (2 oz/60 g) freshly grated Parmesan cheese

2 teaspoons chopped fresh sage

2 cloves garlic

¼ teaspoon salt

Ground black pepper

3 fl oz (90 ml) extra virgin olive oil

CHICKEN

2 teaspoons olive oil

4 boneless, skinless chicken breast halves, about 1 lb (480 g) total

Salt and ground black pepper

4 teaspoons chopped fresh parsley

Preheat an oven to 350°F (180°C). Place walnuts on a baking sheet and bake, stirring occasionally, until nicely toasted, about 10 minutes. Let cool.

For the pesto, place the walnuts, Parmesan cheese, sage, garlic, salt and pepper to taste in a food processor. Pulse until nuts are coarsely ground. Add oil and pulse just until blended, scraping down the sides once with a rubber spatula.

Preheat a two-sided electric indoor grill or ridged grill pan according to the manufacturer's instructions. Rub olive oil over both sides of the chicken and season with salt and pepper.

If using the two-sided grill, place the chicken on the grill, close the cover and cook until the chicken is no longer pink in the center, 4–5 minutes.

If using the grill pan, cook until chicken is no longer pink in the center, 8–10 minutes, turning once midway through the cooking time.

Slice chicken on the diagonal into ½-inch (1-cm) thick strips. Fan out the strips on 4 serving plates and top with a dollop of pesto and a sprinkle of parsley. Serve immediately.

Serves 4

Beef Tenderloin with Horseradish

SAUCE

⅓ cup (3 oz/90 g) sour cream

2 tablespoons mayonnaise

2 tablespoons purchased horseradish

1 teaspoon fresh lemon juice, plus extra as needed

Salt and ground black pepper

BEEF

4 beef tenderloin steaks, cut 1–1¼ inches (2.5–3 cm) thick, about 1–1½ lb (500–750 g) total

Olive oil, for brushing

Salt and ground black pepper

For the sauce, in a small bowl, combine the sour cream, mayonnaise, horseradish and lemon juice; stir until smooth. Add more lemon juice, if needed, and salt and pepper to taste. Cover and refrigerate until needed. (The sauce will keep in the refrigerator for up to 2 days.)

Preheat a two-sided electric indoor grill or ridged grill pan according to the manufacturer's instructions.

Brush both sides of the steaks with the olive oil and season with salt and pepper.

If using the two-sided grill, place the steaks on the grill,

close the cover and cook until the steaks are seared on both sides and done to your liking, 4–5 minutes for medium-rare.

If using the grill pan, sear steaks over high heat for 2–3 minutes per side. Reduce heat to medium and cook until done to your liking, 4–5 minutes more for medium-rare, turning once midway through cooking time.

Serve with horseradish sauce.

Serves 4

Quick Chicken Cacciatore

1 broiler-fryer (roasting) chicken, about 4 lb (1.9 kg), cut into serving pieces

1 yellow onion, thinly sliced

1 green bell pepper, seeded and thinly sliced

1 stalk celery, thinly sliced

3 whole cloves garlic, unpeeled

1 tablespoon olive oil

1 can (28 oz/875 g) chopped tomatoes

¼ cup (2 fl oz/60 ml) dry white wine

½ teaspoon sugar

Salt and ground black pepper

Rinse chicken pieces; pat dry. Reserve wings for another use.

Preheat a large two-sided electric indoor grill according to the manufacturer's instructions.

In a small bowl, toss together the onion, bell pepper, celery, garlic and oil. Arrange chicken, skin-side down, over two-thirds of the grill. Remove garlic cloves from vegetable mixture and place them in the open area of the grill, spooning the remaining vegetables on top. Close cover and cook for 8 minutes.

Toss vegetables, ensuring that garlic remains at the bottom. Continue cooking until chicken is no longer pink in the center and vegetables are browned and tender, about 7 minutes.

Transfer chicken to a serving platter and cover to keep warm.

Scrape cooked vegetables into a medium saucepan, setting garlic cloves aside. Add the tomatoes, wine and sugar and bring to a simmer over medium–high heat.

Meanwhile, squeeze the softened garlic from the skins and mash it into a paste. Add garlic paste to tomato mixture and cook until the mixture is reduced and thickened, about 5 minutes. Season with salt and pepper to taste. Spoon the sauce over the chicken and serve hot.

Serves 4

Ginger-Marinated Steak

2½-inch (6-cm) piece fresh ginger, peeled and sliced

6 cloves garlic

½ cup (4 fl oz/125 ml) dry sherry

¼ cup (2 fl oz/60 ml) soy sauce

2 tablespoons rice wine vinegar

2 tablespoons vegetable oil

1–1½ lb (480–720 g) sirloin, round or flank steak

In a blender or food processor, pulse the ginger and garlic until coarsely chopped. Add sherry, soy sauce, vinegar and oil and pulse just to combine.

Place the steak in a large resealable plastic bag or shallow, nonaluminum dish; pour in the marinade and turn steak to coat. Cover the dish, if using, and refrigerate for at least 6 hours or overnight.

Preheat a two-sided electric indoor grill or ridged grill pan according to the manufacturer's instructions.

Remove steak from marinade, shaking off the excess.

If using the two-sided grill, place the steak on the grill, close the cover and cook until done to your liking, about 8 minutes for medium-rare for a 1¼-inch (3-cm) thick steak.

If using the grill pan, cook the steak until done to your liking, about 18 minutes for medium-rare for a 1¼-inch (3-cm) thick steak, turning it once midway through the cooking time.

Transfer the steak to a cutting board and let it stand for a few minutes before slicing thinly across the grain to serve.

Serves 4

Turkey Breast with Spinach Couscous

1 boneless, skinless turkey breast half, about 2 lb (960 g)

Olive oil

Salt and ground black pepper

8 oz (240 g) fresh spinach leaves, washed, dried and stemmed

½ cup (4 fl oz/125 ml) water

⅓ cup (2 oz/60 g) instant couscous

2 tablespoons olive oil

¼ cup (1 oz/30 g) pine nuts

1 teaspoon minced garlic

½ teaspoon salt

¼ teaspoon ground black pepper

1 teaspoon fresh lemon juice

½ teaspoon grated lemon zest

1 large egg, lightly beaten

Place turkey, smooth side up, on a work surface. Trim away any fat. Cover with plastic wrap and gently pound with a meat mallet to flatten the meat into a more even layer. (If the small tenderloin separates, don't worry; it will meld back together during cooking.) With a knife held parallel to the work surface, and working from the thinner toward the thicker edge, cut a pocket in the breast, leaving the thicker edge intact. Open the breast out for stuffing.

For the stuffing, coarsely chop the spinach and set aside. In a small saucepan, bring the water to a boil. Stir in the couscous, remove from the heat, cover and let stand for 3 minutes. Fluff the couscous with a fork.

In a large frying pan, heat the olive oil over medium heat. Add the pine nuts and cook, stirring, until they begin to color, about 30 seconds. Add the garlic and continue to stir until the pine nuts are golden and the garlic is fragrant, about 30 seconds more. Add this mixture to the couscous.

Return the pan to the heat, add the spinach, and stir until it is just wilted, about 2 minutes. Remove from heat and stir in the salt, pepper, lemon juice, lemon zest and the reserved couscous mixture. Stir in the egg.

Preheat a large two-sided electric indoor grill according to the manufacturer's instructions.

Spread the stuffing over half of the turkey breast in an even layer. Fold the other half firmly over the filling. Rub the top with olive oil and season with salt and pepper to taste.

Place the turkey on the grill, close the cover, and cook until it is no longer pink in the center, about 8 minutes.

Transfer the turkey to a cutting board and let it stand for a few minutes. Cut crosswise into thick slices and serve.

Serves 4 to 6

Flank Steak Pinwheels

2 tablespoons olive oil

1 small red bell pepper, seeded and finely chopped

1 jalapeño chili, seeded and finely chopped

1 teaspoon finely chopped garlic

1 teaspoon ground cumin

1 tablespoon tomato paste

1 cup (6 oz/185 g) fresh or frozen corn kernels

2 tablespoons pitted and chopped black olives

1/2 teaspoon dried oregano

1/2 teaspoon salt

1 piece flank steak, about 1 1/2 lb (720 g)

Salt and ground black pepper

For the stuffing, in a frying pan, heat the olive oil over medium-high heat. Add the bell pepper and the jalapeño and cook, stirring, until softened, about 3 minutes. Add the garlic and cumin and cook until fragrant, about 30 seconds more.

Remove frying pan from heat; add tomato paste and mash with a spoon until it is blended into the mixture. Add corn, olives, oregano and salt; stir well. Set aside to cool completely.

Place steak between two large sheets of plastic wrap. With a meat mallet, pound it into a thinner layer of even thickness.

Press corn mixture firmly and evenly over steak. Starting with a wide edge, roll steak and filling up together. Lightly score the top of the rolled steak to mark it into 8 equal sections. Tie a piece of cooking twine firmly around the center of each of the sections. Season the outside of the roll with salt and pepper. Cut the roll crosswise on the score marks into 8 pieces.

Preheat a large two-sided electric indoor grill or ridged grill pan according to the manufacturer's instructions.

If using the two-sided grill, arrange the spirals on the grill cut side down, close the cover and cook until done to your liking, about 4 minutes for medium-rare.

If using the grill pan, place the spirals on the pan cut side down, and cook until done to your liking, about 7 minutes for medium-rare, turning them carefully midway through the cooking time.

Divide the pinwheels among 4 plates and serve.

Serves 4

Duck with Cranberry–Pear Sauce

2 teaspoons canola oil

1 large golden (French) shallot, finely chopped

1½ teaspoons chopped fresh rosemary

2 cups (8 oz/240 g) fresh or frozen cranberries

⅓ cup (2 oz/60 g) diced dried pears

1 cup (8 fl oz/240 ml) water

½ cup (3½ oz/105 g) brown sugar

1 tablespoon balsamic vinegar

Freshly ground black pepper

2 teaspoons olive oil

4 boneless duck breast halves, about 1½ lb (720 g) total

Salt and ground black pepper

For the sauce, in a medium saucepan, heat canola oil over medium–high heat. Add shallot and sauté until softened, about 3 minutes. Add rosemary and cook, stirring, about 30 seconds more. Stir in cranberries, pear, water, sugar, vinegar and pepper to taste and bring the mixture to a boil. Lower the heat slightly and boil, stirring frequently, for 10 minutes. Set aside.

Preheat a two-sided electric indoor grill or ridged grill pan according to the manufacturer's instructions.

Rub olive oil over both sides of the duck breasts and season with salt and pepper to taste.

If using the two-sided grill, place the duck breasts on the grill, close the cover and cook until done to your liking, about 4 minutes for medium-rare.

If using the grill pan, place the duck on the pan, skin-side down, and cook until it is well browned on the bottom, about 6 minutes. Turn and cook until done to your liking, 2–3 minutes more for medium-rare.

Divide among 4 plates and spoon sauce over and around the duck. Serve immediately.

Serves 4

Pork with Cider–Molasses Sauce

1 teaspoon canola oil

1 large clove garlic, minced

1 jalapeño chili, seeded and minced

1 cup (8 fl oz/240 ml) apple cider

⅓ cup (4 oz/120 g) molasses

¼ cup (2 fl oz/60 ml) cider vinegar

Salt and ground black pepper

2 teaspoons chili powder

1½ teaspoons coarse salt

2 small pork tenderloins, about ¾ lb (375 g) each, trimmed of excess fat

For the sauce, in a medium saucepan, heat the canola oil over medium–low heat. Add the garlic and jalapeño and cook, stirring, for about 30 seconds. Stir in the cider, molasses and vinegar and bring to a boil. Lower the heat and simmer until thickened to a syrup consistency, about 20 minutes. Add salt and pepper to taste. Cover the sauce and set aside.

Preheat a two-sided electric indoor grill or ridged grill pan according to the manufacturer's instructions.

Combine the chili powder and salt and rub the mixture all over the pork tenderloins.

If using the two-sided grill, place pork on grill, close cover, and cook until just slightly pink in the center, about 8 minutes.

If using the grill pan, cook the pork until just slightly pink in the center, about 15 minutes, turning it once midway through the cooking time.

Transfer pork to a cutting board and let stand for 5 minutes.

Cut the pork crosswise into ½- to ¾-inch (10-mm–2-cm) slices. Divide among 4 plates and spoon the sauce over the pork. Serve immediately.

Serves 4

Turkish Meatballs in Pita Bread

MINTED YOGURT SAUCE

2 cups (1 lb/480 g) plain (natural) yogurt

1 clove garlic, minced

2 tablespoons (1 fl oz/30 ml) olive oil

1½ teaspoons red wine vinegar or fresh lemon juice

1 tablespoon chopped fresh parsley

1 tablespoon chopped fresh mint

MEATBALLS AND SANDWICHES

1 lb (480 g) ground (minced) lamb

1 large egg, lightly beaten

1 small yellow onion, grated

1 clove garlic, finely chopped

1½ teaspoons chopped fresh thyme

½ teaspoon salt

¼ teaspoon ground black pepper

4 pita bread rounds, sliced in halves horizontally

8 slices tomato

4 slices red (Spanish) onion

For the sauce, line a strainer with cheesecloth (muslin) or several moistened paper coffee filters. Set it over a bowl, add the yogurt, cover and refrigerate for 4–6 hours, or until yogurt has drained, thickened and reduced to about 1 cup (8 oz/240 g).

Discard the drained liquid. In a small bowl, stir together the thickened yogurt, the garlic, oil, vinegar or lemon juice, parsley and mint. Add salt and pepper to taste. Cover and refrigerate.

For the meatballs, in a bowl, combine the lamb, egg, onion, garlic, thyme, salt and pepper. Mix with your hands until well combined, then shape into sixteen 1½-inch (4-cm) balls.

Preheat a two-sided electric indoor grill or ridged grill pan according to the manufacturer's instructions.

If using the two-sided grill, place the meatballs on the grill, close the cover, and cook until they are no longer pink in the center, about 3 minutes.

If using the grill pan, cook until the meatballs are no longer pink in the center, about 5 minutes, turning several times during cooking to brown on all sides.

Serve meatballs in pita breads with the sliced tomato and onion and the yogurt sauce.

Serves 4

Pork Chops with Apple–Raisin Relish

2 teaspoons olive oil

1 small clove garlic, minced

2 Granny Smith apples, unpeeled, cored and diced

1 cup (8 fl oz/240 ml) orange juice

1/3 cup (2 oz/60 g) golden raisins (sultanas)

2 teaspoons cider vinegar

1/2 teaspoon chopped fresh chili

1/4 teaspoon ground cumin

1/8 teaspoon salt

Ground black pepper, to taste

4 bone-in center-cut pork chops, 1/2 inch (1 cm) thick, about 1 1/2 lb (750 g) total

2 teaspoons olive oil

Salt and ground black pepper

For the relish, in a nonstick frying pan, heat the oil over medium–high heat. Add garlic and cook, stirring constantly, for 20 seconds. Add the apples and sauté until softened slightly, about 3 minutes.

Add orange juice, raisins, vinegar, chili, cumin, salt and pepper. Cook, stirring occasionally, until mixture has reduced to a sauce consistency, about 8 minutes. Taste and add more salt and pepper if needed. Keep warm.

Preheat a two-sided electric indoor grill or ridged grill pan according to the manufacturer's instructions.

Rub both sides of the pork chops with the olive oil and season with salt and pepper.

If using the two-sided grill, place the chops on the grill, close the cover, and cook until just a trace of pink remains in the center, 2 1/2–3 minutes.

If using the grill pan, cook the chops until just a trace of pink remains in the center, 4–6 minutes, turning once midway through cooking time.

Divide chops among 4 plates and spoon the relish over the top. Serve immediately.

Serves 4

Grilled Lamb Sandwiches

MARINADE AND LAMB

1/4 cup (2 fl oz/60 ml) red wine vinegar

2 tablespoons olive oil

4 cloves garlic, chopped

1 teaspoon chopped fresh rosemary

1/4 teaspoon ground black pepper

1 teaspoon salt, or to taste

1 1/4 lb (625 g) lamb steak, cut from the leg

SAUCE

1/3 cup (3 oz/85 g) mayonnaise (regular or reduced fat)

2 tablespoons plain (natural) yogurt

2 teaspoons Dijon mustard

1/2 teaspoon chopped fresh rosemary

Ground black pepper

TO ASSEMBLE

8 slices sourdough bread, about 1/2 inch (1 cm) thick

3 tablespoons olive oil

1 cup (1 oz/30 g) watercress or arugula leaves

In a shallow, nonaluminum dish, combine the vinegar, oil, garlic, rosemary, pepper and salt. Add lamb and turn to coat. Cover; and refrigerate for 2–24 hours.

Whisk together all the sauce ingredients until smooth. Cover and refrigerate for at least 1 hour.

Preheat a two-sided electric indoor grill or ridged grill pan according to the manufacturer's instructions.

Remove lamb from marinade, shaking off the excess.

If using the two-sided grill, place lamb on grill, close cover, and cook until done to your liking, about 4 minutes for medium-rare.

If using the grill pan, cook the lamb until done to your liking, 8–10 minutes for medium-rare, turning once midway through cooking time.

Transfer lamb to a cutting board and let stand for 5 minutes.

Brush bread on both sides with olive oil. Grill until browned, about 1 minute on the two-sided grill or 1½–2 minutes per side in the grill pan.

Thinly slice the lamb across the grain. Spread some of the sauce onto half of the bread slices. Top with the lamb, salad leaves and the remaining bread.

Serves 4

SEAFOOD

Shrimp with Prosciutto and Zucchini

MARINADE

2 tablespoons fruity Italian white wine

2 tablespoons olive oil

1 tablespoon fresh lemon juice

8 strips lemon zest, each about 2 inches (5 cm) long

3 large cloves garlic, minced

1 teaspoon fresh thyme leaves or 1/2 teaspoon dried thyme

1/2 teaspoon crumbled bay leaf

Ground black pepper

SKEWERS

16 large shrimp (prawns), about 1 lb (480 g) total, peeled and deveined

2 medium zucchini (courgettes), trimmed and cut lengthwise into slices 1/8-inch (3-mm) thick

8 slices prosciutto, cut paper thin, trimmed of excess fat and cut in halves lengthwise

For the marinade, in a shallow, nonaluminum dish, combine all the marinade ingredients and mix well. Add the shrimp and turn them to coat. Cover dish and refrigerate for 30 minutes to 2 hours.

Preheat a two-sided electric indoor grill or ridged grill pan according to the manufacturer's instructions.

If using the two-sided grill, arrange the zucchini slices on the grill, close the cover, and cook just until soft and pliable, about 3 minutes. Cool slightly.

Remove shrimp from marinade, reserving lemon strips. Wrap 1 slice of prosciutto around a shrimp, then wrap it with a zucchini slice. Thread shrimp onto a skewer. Repeat with the remaining shrimp, prosciutto and zucchini, putting 4 shrimp on each skewer. Thread 2 lemon strips on each skewer.

Place the skewers on the grill, close the cover, and cook until the shrimp is just cooked through, about 3 minutes.

SHRIMP WITH PROSCIUTTO AND ZUCCHINI

If using the grill pan, cook the zucchini slices, in batches as necessary, until just soft and pliable, about 5 minutes, turning once midway through cooking time. Cool slightly.

Prepare skewers as described above. Cook until the shrimp is just cooked through, about 6 minutes, turning once midway through cooking time.

Arrange the skewers on a platter and serve immediately.

Serves 4

Tuna Steaks with Onion Marmalade

4 oz (120 g) pancetta or thickly sliced bacon

1/4 cup (2 fl oz/60 ml) olive oil, plus 2 tablespoons extra

2 large white onions, thinly sliced

1/2 cup (4 fl oz/120 ml) balsamic vinegar

1/4 cup (2 fl oz/60 ml) sherry vinegar

1/2 cup (4 fl oz/120 ml) water

Salt and ground white pepper

2 teaspoons sugar

1/2 teaspoon cayenne pepper

4 tuna steaks, 5 oz (150 g) each

For the marmalade, cut the pancetta or bacon crosswise into strips 1/2 inch (10 mm) thick.

In a sauté pan over high heat, warm the 1/4 cup (2 fl oz/60 ml) olive oil. Add the pancetta or bacon and sauté until slightly crisp, about 2 minutes. Add the sliced onions and continue to sauté until the onions are golden brown, about 10 minutes.

Stir in the balsamic vinegar, sherry vinegar, water, 1 teaspoon salt, 1/4 teaspoon white pepper, sugar and cayenne. Bring to a boil over medium heat, then continue to boil until all liquid has evaporated, 12–15 minutes.

About 5 minutes before the marmalade is ready, cook the tuna steaks. In a separate sauté pan over high heat, warm the 2 tablespoons olive oil. Sprinkle both sides of the tuna steaks with salt and white pepper to taste. Place the steaks in the hot pan and cook, turning once, until done to your liking, 1–2 minutes on each side for medium-rare, depending upon the thickness of the steaks.

Transfer the tuna steaks to warmed individual plates. Top with the onion marmalade and serve immediately.

Serves 4

Grilled Bluefish and Potatoes

1–1½ lb (480–720 g) bluefish fillets, cut into 4 pieces

Salt and ground black pepper

3 fl oz (90 ml) olive oil

1½ tablespoons fresh lemon juice

2 teaspoons chopped fresh rosemary

1 lb (480 g) boiling potatoes, unpeeled, cut into ¼-inch (5-mm) thick slices

1½ teaspoons chopped fresh garlic

½ teaspoon salt

Season both sides of the fish fillets with salt and pepper.

In a shallow, nonaluminum dish, combine 3 tablespoons of the olive oil with the lemon juice and rosemary. Add the fish fillets and turn to coat well. Cover the dish and refrigerate for 1 hour.

Preheat a large two-sided electric indoor grill according to the manufacturer's instructions.

In a bowl, combine potatoes, garlic, salt, and the remaining 2 tablespoons of olive oil.

Spread the potato slices evenly over the grill, close the cover, and cook for 6 minutes. Open the grill and turn the potatoes

over with tongs. Continue cooking until the potatoes are tender, about 6 minutes more. Open the grill and place the fish fillets, skin side down, on top of the potatoes, pouring any juices from the dish over them. Cook until the fish is opaque in the center, 3–5 minutes. (They will need 2–3 minutes per ½ inch/ 10 mm of thickness.)

Divide the fish and potatoes among 4 plates and serve immediately.

Serves 4

Salmon with Maple–Balsamic Glaze

GLAZE

½ cup (4 fl oz/120 ml) balsamic vinegar

¼ cup (2 fl oz/60 ml) maple syrup

3 tablespoons rice wine vinegar

½ teaspoon salt

¼ teaspoon ground black pepper

SALMON

1 center-cut skinless salmon fillet, about 1½ lb (720 g) total, cut into 4 pieces

Salt and ground black pepper

For glaze, in a small saucepan, combine all glaze ingredients. Bring to a boil over high heat and cook, stirring, until the mixture is syrupy and reduced to about ½ cup (4 fl oz/120 ml), about 6 minutes. Set aside.

Preheat a two-sided electric indoor grill or ridged grill pan according to the manufacturer's instructions.

To prepare the salmon, remove any bones and season both sides with salt and pepper.

If using the two-sided grill, place the fish on the grill, close the cover and cook until the fillets are golden on the outside

and just cooked through, about 3 minutes. (They will need 2–3 minutes per ½ inch/10 mm of thickness.)

If using the grill pan, cook the fish until the fillets are golden on the outside and just cooked through, about 6 minutes, turning once midway through the cooking time. (They will need 4–6 minutes per ½ inch/ 10 mm of thickness.)

Serve each fillet drizzled with the glaze.

Serves 4

Grilled Shrimp with Mango Salsa

SHRIMP

¼ cup (2 fl oz/60 ml) olive oil

3 cloves garlic, thinly sliced

3 tablespoons fresh lime juice

Salt and ground black pepper

1½ lb (720 g) large shrimp (prawns), peeled and deveined

SALSA

2 ripe mangoes, peeled and diced

4 green (spring) onions, white and green parts, thinly sliced

1 small hot chili, seeded and very finely chopped

2–3 tablespoons chopped cilantro (fresh coriander)

2 tablespoons fresh lime juice

Lime wedges, for garnish

To prepare the shrimp, in a small saucepan, heat the olive oil and garlic over low heat until fragrant, about 3 minutes. Transfer to a medium bowl.

Stir in lime juice, ½ teaspoon salt, and ¼ teaspoon pepper. Cool slightly. Add shrimp and stir to coat well. Marinate the shrimp at room temperature for 30 minutes, stirring occasionally.

Meanwhile, for the salsa, combine mango, green onion, chili, cilantro and lime juice. Add salt to taste and set aside.

Preheat a large two-sided electric indoor grill or ridged grill pan according to the manufacturer's instructions.

Thread shrimp onto skewers, passing the skewer through points near both the head and tail sections, leaving a little space between the pieces.

If using the two-sided grill, place the skewers on the grill, close the cover, and cook, in batches as necessary, until the shrimp turn pink and are opaque throughout, 2–3 minutes.

If using the grill pan, cook the shrimp, in batches as necessary, until they turn pink and are opaque throughout, 4–6 minutes, turning once midway through the cooking time.

Serve with salsa and lime.

Serves 4

Stuffed Squid

12 medium or 16 small squid

BREAD CRUMB FILLING

3 tablespoons olive oil, plus extra for brushing

1½ cups (6 oz/180 g) chopped onion

4 cloves garlic, minced

3 oz (90 g) chopped serrano, prosciutto or similar cured ham (optional)

1–1½ cups (2–3 oz/60–90 g) fresh bread crumbs

¼ cup (2 fl oz/60 ml) fresh lemon juice

¼ cup (⅓ oz/10 g) chopped fresh flat-leaf (Italian) parsley

Salt and ground black pepper

DRESSING

⅓ cup (3 fl oz/80 ml) extra virgin olive oil

3–4 tablespoons fresh lemon juice

3 tablespoons dried oregano

To clean each squid, grip the head and pull it and the attached innards gently but firmly from the body. Using your fingertips, squeeze out the small, round beak from the mouth at the base of the tentacles. Using a sharp knife, cut away the eyes. Reserve the tentacles. Using your fingers, clean out the body pouch under running water, being careful not to tear it. Remove and discard the transparent quill-like cartilage from along one side of the pouch. Rub off the filmy brownish skin from the body and rinse the tentacles and body well. Chop the tentacles and set the bodies and tentacles aside.

Prepare a fire in a charcoal grill or preheat a gas grill to medium-high heat.

For the bread crumb filling, in a sauté pan over medium heat, warm the 3 tablespoons olive oil. Add onion and sauté until tender, 8–10 minutes.

Add the garlic, ham (if using), chopped tentacles and enough of the bread crumbs to bind the mixture together. Sauté over medium heat for 2 minutes. Stir in the lemon juice and parsley and add salt and pepper to taste. Let cool.

Carefully stuff the bread crumb mixture into the squid bodies

and skewer the ends closed with toothpicks. Thread the squid crosswise onto long metal skewers. Brush them with olive oil and sprinkle with salt and pepper. Place on grill rack and cook, turning once, until the squid are tender and opaque, about 3 minutes per side.

Meanwhile, make the dressing. In a small bowl, whisk together the olive oil, lemon juice and oregano.

Slide the squid off the skewers onto a warmed platter, drizzle the dressing evenly over the top and serve hot.

Serves 4

Grilled Mullet with Thyme

6 red mullet, about 6 oz (180 g) each, cleaned

1/4 cup (2 fl oz/60 ml) extra virgin olive oil

12 sprigs fresh thyme

12 slices lemon

Salt and ground black pepper

Clean and wash the fish.

Prepare a fire in a charcoal grill or preheat a gas grill to medium-high heat.

Oil 6 sheets of foil; place a fish on each sheet. Place 1 thyme sprig and 1 lemon slice inside each fish. Lay 1 lemon slice and 1 thyme sprig on top of each fish; season with salt and pepper to taste.

Close up the packages, rolling edges of foil together to seal. Place on the grill rack and cook until fish is opaque throughout, about 5 minutes on each side.

Serves 6

Trout with Olives and Chili

½ cup (4 fl oz/120 ml) olive oil

¾ cup (6 fl oz/180 ml) coconut milk

¼ cup (2 fl oz/60 ml) lime juice

2 hot red chilies, chopped

½ cup (3 oz/90 g) stuffed olives

1 onion, chopped

¼ cup (⅓ oz/10 g) chopped mint leaves

2 limes, each cut into 8 slices

8 small trout, cleaned

Serves 8

In a shallow dish, combine the oil, coconut milk, lime juice, chilies, olives, onion and mint. Add the lime slices and trout. Cover and refrigerate for at least 4 hours.

Prepare a fire in a charcoal grill or preheat a gas grill to medium-high heat.

When ready to barbecue, oil 8 sheets of foil. Place a fish on each sheet and top with 2 tablespoons of marinade and 2 lime slices. Close up the packages, rolling edges of foil together to seal. Place on the grill rack and cook until the fish is opaque throughout, about 8 minutes on each side. Serve at once.

Grilled Fish Tacos

SAUCE

⅓ cup (3 oz/90 g) mayonnaise

⅓ cup (3 fl oz/90 ml) sour cream or yogurt

¼ cup (1 oz/90 g) chopped red (Spanish) onion

¼ cup (⅓ oz/10 g) chopped cilantro (fresh coriander)

TACOS

1 tablespoon olive oil

1 teaspoon hot chili powder

¼ teaspoon salt

8 large or 12 small corn tortillas

1 lb (480 g) white fish fillets, such as pollock, red snapper, haddock, halibut, mahi mahi or cod

TO SERVE

2 cups (6 oz/180 g) shredded green cabbage

1 cup (8 fl oz/240 ml) Quick Tomato Salsa (page 77) or purchased tomato salsa

2 avocados, pitted, peeled and sliced

2 limes, cut into wedges

For the sauce, in a small bowl, whisk together the mayonnaise, sour cream or yogurt, onion, and cilantro.

In a medium bowl, whisk together the olive oil, chili powder and salt; set aside.

Preheat oven to 300°F (150°C). Preheat a large two-sided electric indoor grill or large grill pan according to the manufacturer's instructions.

Directly on top of electric or gas stove burners, lightly toast both sides of the tortillas. Wrap them in foil and put in the oven to keep warm.

Cut the fish fillets crosswise into 1-inch (2.5-cm) wide strips. Add the fish to the reserved olive oil mixture and toss to coat evenly.

If using the two-sided grill, arrange the fish pieces in an even layer on the grill, close the cover, and cook until the fish is just opaque in the center, about 2 minutes, depending on the type of fish. Transfer to a platter.

If using the grill pan, arrange the fish pieces in an even layer and cook until just opaque in the center, about 4 minutes, depending on the type of fish. Turn once midway through the cooking time. Transfer to a platter.

To assemble, put a few table-spoons of cabbage in the middle of a tortilla, top with some of the fish, a spoonful of sauce, a spoonful of salsa, some avocado slices and a squeeze of lime juice. Fold up and eat.

Serves 4

Grilled Swordfish Kabobs

½ cup (4 fl oz / 120 ml) olive oil

6 tablespoons (3 fl oz / 90 ml) fresh lemon juice

1 teaspoon paprika

2 bay leaves, crushed, plus 12 whole bay leaves

2 lb (980 g) swordfish fillets, cut into 1¼-inch (3-cm) cubes

2 lemons, thinly sliced, plus extra lemon wedges, to serve

2 green bell peppers (capsicums), seeded, deribbed and cut into 1¼-inch (3-cm) squares

16 ripe but firm cherry tomatoes

Salt and ground black pepper

In a shallow nonaluminum bowl, whisk together the olive oil, lemon juice, paprika and crushed bay leaves. Add the swordfish cubes and turn to coat. Cover and marinate in the refrigerator for about 4 hours.

Prepare a fire in a charcoal grill or preheat a gas grill to medium-high heat.

Remove the fish cubes from the marinade, reserving marinade.

Thread the cubes onto metal skewers, alternating them with the whole bay leaves, lemon slices, bell pepper pieces and cherry tomatoes. Sprinkle with salt and pepper.

Place the skewers on an oiled grill rack and cook, turning as needed and basting a few times with the reserved marinade, until the fish is opaque throughout, about 10 minutes.

Transfer the skewers to a warmed platter and serve hot with lemon wedges.

Serves 4

Sea Bass in Thai Coconut Sauce

1½ tablespoons canola oil

2 large purple (Asian) shallots, finely chopped

3 cloves garlic, finely chopped

1 stalk fresh lemongrass, trimmed and coarsely chopped

1 tablespoon green curry paste

2 teaspoons grated lime zest

2 cans (each 14 oz/420 ml) unsweetened coconut milk

1½ lb (720 g) sea bass fillet, cut into 4 pieces

2 tablespoons fresh lime juice

2 tablespoons coarsely chopped cilantro (fresh coriander)

Salt and ground black pepper

For the sauce, in a large saucepan, heat the oil over medium heat. Add the shallots and garlic and cook, stirring constantly, for 1 minute. Add the lemongrass and stir for 1 minute more. Add the curry paste and lime zest, then gradually stir in the coconut milk. Bring to a boil, lower the heat, and simmer slowly until the mixture is very fragrant and thickened slightly, about 15 minutes. Set the sauce aside to cool completely.

Place the fish in a shallow, nonreactive dish just large enough to hold the pieces in a single layer. Pour about half of the sauce over the fish pieces and turn them to coat well. Cover the dish and refrigerate for 1 hour. Strain the remaining sauce into a clean saucepan.

Preheat a two-sided electric indoor grill or ridged grill pan according to the manufacturer's instructions.

Heat the strained sauce over low heat. Drain fish from marinade, wiping off excess. Discard the marinade. Season all sides of the fish with salt and pepper.

If using the two-sided grill, arrange the fish on the grill, close the cover, and cook until the fish is just cooked through, 2–3 minutes. (It will need

SEA BASS IN THAI COCONUT SAUCE

2–3 minutes per per $1/2$ inch/
10 mm of thickness.)

If using the grill pan, cook
the fish until it is just cooked
through, 4–6 minutes, turning
once midway through cooking
time. (It will need 4–6 minutes
per $1/2$ inch/10 mm of thickness.)

Remove the sauce from the
heat, stir in the lime juice and
cilantro, and add salt and
pepper to taste. Divide the fish
among 4 serving plates and
spoon the sauce over the top.

Serve immediately.

Serves 4

Fish in Grape Leaves

¼ cup (2 fl oz/60 ml) olive oil

2 tablespoons chopped fresh parsley or fennel

2 teaspoons chopped fresh thyme or oregano

Juice of 1 small lemon

½ teaspoon salt

¼ teaspoon ground black pepper

2 lb (980 g) fresh large sardines, cleaned with heads left on, or 4 white fish fillets, such as cod, sea bass or hake, about 6 oz (180 g) each

Bottled grape leaves, rinsed, stems removed

Lemon wedges, for garnish

In a shallow, nonaluminum dish, whisk together the olive oil, parsley or fennel, thyme or oregano, lemon juice, salt and pepper. Add the fish, turning to coat well. Let marinate at room temperature for 1–2 hours.

Prepare a fire in a charcoal grill or preheat a gas grill to medium-high heat.

Remove fish from marinade, shaking off the excess. Wrap each fillet in 1 or 2 grape leaves, leaving exposed the head and tail of each fish or both ends of each fillet; secure leaves with toothpicks, if needed.

Place the fish packets on the grill rack and cook until opaque throughout, 7–10 minutes on each side for whole fish and 5–6 minutes on each side for fish fillets. Turn once midway through cooking time.

Transfer to warmed plates and serve hot with lemon wedges.

Serves 4

Citrus Swordfish with Spinach

¼ cup (2 fl oz/60 ml) water

¼ cup (2 oz/60 g) unsalted butter

3 fl oz (90 ml) olive oil

1¼ lb (600 g) spinach leaves, stems removed, leaves carefully washed

Salt and ground black pepper

4 swordfish steaks, about 5 oz (150 g) each

Juice of ½ orange

Juice of ½ lemon

Juice of ¼ grapefruit

¼ cup (2 fl oz/60 ml) veal stock or chicken stock

In a large saucepan over high heat, combine the water, butter and 2 tablespoons of the olive oil. Once the butter has melted completely, add the spinach leaves and salt and pepper to taste. Cover and cook, stirring every 20–30 seconds, until wilted, about 2 minutes. Remove from heat, cover and set aside.

In a large sauté pan over high heat, warm 1 tablespoon of the remaining oil. Sprinkle both sides of the swordfish steaks with salt and pepper to taste. Place the fish in the hot pan and cook, turning once, until done to your liking, 1–2 minutes on

each side for medium-rare. Transfer the fish to a plate and cover to keep warm.

In a small bowl, combine the citrus juices.

Pour off any oil remaining in the sauté pan and place pan over high heat. When hot, pour in the citrus juices and deglaze by stirring to dislodge any browned bits from the bottom of the pan. Boil until the liquid is reduced by half, then add the veal or chicken stock and salt and pepper to taste. Return to a boil and stir in the remaining olive oil. Remove from the heat.

Drain the spinach and divide among warmed individual plates. Place the fish steaks on top of the spinach and spoon the citrus mixture evenly over the fish. Serve immediately.

Serves 4

Spicy Barbecued Snapper with Dill

1 or 2 snapper or bream,
about 2 lb (980 g) total weight

Salt and ground black pepper

2 tablespoons (1 oz/30 g) butter,
or olive or vegetable oil

1 lemon, thinly sliced

3–4 sprigs fresh dill

Prepare a fire in a charcoal grill or preheat a gas grill to medium-high heat.

Clean the fish and make several diagonal slashes on each side.

Season inside and out with salt and pepper. Oil or butter 1 or 2 squares of aluminum foil and place the fish on the foil.

Place several lemon slices and a sprig or two of dill in the cavity of the fish. Arrange the remaining lemon slices over fish.

Wrap the foil around the fish, folding the edges over to seal. Place on the grill rack over moderate heat and cook for about 25 minutes for 1 large fish and 15 minutes for 2 smaller fish. Test during cooking by inserting a skewer into the thickest part of the fish. If the flesh is tender and opaque throughout, the fish is done.

Serves 4

Sardines with Garlic Oil Dressing

12 fresh sardines

1½ teaspoons coarse salt

3 tablespoons vegetable or olive oil

3–4 cloves garlic, finely chopped

Fresh herbs of your choice, such as dill, chives, basil, flat-leaf (Italian) parsley and/or coriander

Lemon slices, for garnish

Sprinkle the sardines with salt about 20 minutes before cooking.

Prepare a fire in a charcoal grill or preheat a gas grill to medium-high heat.

Brush the sardines with oil and cook on a barbecue rack until just cooked through.

Meanwhile, in a small pan, heat the remaining oil and add the garlic. Pour the hot garlic oil over the fish, garnish with herbs and lemon, and serve at once.

Serves 4

Tuna Burgers

MAYONNAISE

2 teaspoons wasabi powder

2 teaspoons water

½ cup (4 oz/120 g) mayonnaise (regular or reduced fat)

BURGERS

1 lb (480 g) fresh tuna

4 green (spring) onions, finely chopped

1 clove garlic, finely chopped

4 teaspoons grated fresh ginger

4 teaspoons soy sauce

2 teaspoons Dijon mustard

2 teaspoons mayonnaise

4 teaspoons olive oil

4 hamburger buns

For the mayonnaise, in a small bowl, stir together the wasabi powder and water. Stir in the mayonnaise. Let the mixture stand for at least 20 minutes.

Using a sharp knife, chop the tuna until it resembles ground beef (this will take a few minutes; do not use a food processor). In a bowl, combine the tuna, green onions, garlic, ginger, soy sauce, mustard and mayonnaise. Form the mixture into four 1-inch (2.5-cm)-thick patties. Brush on both sides with the olive oil.

Preheat a two-sided electric indoor grill or ridged grill pan according to the manufacturer's instructions.

If using the two-sided grill, place patties on grill, close cover, and cook until nicely browned on the outside and still slightly pink in the center, 1–1½ minutes.

If using the grill pan, cook the tuna patties until nicely browned on the outside and still slightly pink in the center, 2–4 minutes, turning once midway through the cooking time.

While the tuna burgers are cooking, toast the buns. Spread the toasted buns generously with the wasabi mayonnaise, place a tuna patty on each one, and serve immediately.

Serves 4

Halibut with Tomato Sauce

SAUCE

1 tablespoon canola oil

1 onion, finely chopped

3 cloves garlic, minced

1 can (14 oz/420 g) tomatoes, drained and chopped

½ cup (2½ oz/75 g) green olives, pitted and sliced

¼ cup (1½ oz/45 g) dried currants or raisins

⅓ cup (3 fl oz/90 ml) water

1 teaspoon chopped fresh oregano, or ¼ teaspoon dried

Salt and ground black pepper

2 tablespoons chopped cilantro (fresh coriander) or parsley

1 tablespoon fresh lime or lemon juice

FISH

1½ lb (720 g) halibut steak, cut into 4 pieces

Canola oil

Salt and ground black pepper

Lime or lemon wedges, for garnish

To make the sauce, in a large skillet heat the oil over medium heat. Add the onion and cook, stirring, until softened, about 5 minutes. Add garlic and stir until fragrant, about 1 minute more. Add the tomatoes, olives, currants or raisins, water and oregano.

Reduce the heat to low, cover the skillet and simmer, stirring occasionally, until the tomatoes have softened into a sauce, about 10 minutes. Add salt and pepper to taste. (If making sauce ahead of time, prepare it to this stage, cover, and refrigerate for up to 2 days. Reheat it before continuing.) Add the cilantro or

223

parsley and lime or lemon juice. Keep the sauce warm.

Preheat a two-sided electric indoor grill or ridged grill pan according to the manufacturer's instructions.

Brush the halibut pieces with oil and season with salt and pepper.

If using the two-sided grill, place fish on grill, close cover, and cook until it is browned and crisp on top and opaque in the center, 4–7 minutes. (It will need 2–3 minutes per ½ inch/ 10 mm of thickness.)

If using the grill pan, cook the fish until it is browned and crisp

on top and opaque in the center, 8–10 minutes. (It will need 4–6 minutes per ½ inch/10 mm of thickness.) Turn the fish once midway through cooking time.

Transfer the fish to warmed plates and spoon the warm sauce over the top.

Serves 4

Fish in a Cloak

1 sea bream, porgy, dentex, sea bass, salmon or grouper, about 4 lb (1.9 kg)

½ cup (4 fl oz / 120 ml) vinegar

½ cup (4 fl oz / 120 ml) dry white wine

1 teaspoon whole black peppercorns

2 hardboiled egg yolks, chopped

1 tablespoon chopped fresh flat-leaf (Italian) parsley

Juice of 1 lemon

⅓ cup (3 fl oz / 90 ml) extra virgin olive oil

Salt

Clean the fish and place it in a deep dish. Pour the vinegar and wine over it, sprinkle with peppercorns and leave to marinate for about 3 hours.

Prepare a fire in a charcoal grill or preheat a gas grill to medium-high heat.

Drain and dry the fish. Grill until just cooked through, 10–15 minutes on each side.

Combine the egg yolks, parsley, lemon juice, oil and salt to taste. Transfer fish to a serving plate and serve the sauce separately.

Serves 6

Grilled Salmon Trout

6 salmon trout steaks, about 6 oz (180 g) each

¼ cup (2 fl oz/60 ml) extra virgin olive oil

Salt and ground black pepper

Juice of 1 lemon

¼ cup (2 fl oz/60 ml) dry white wine

1 tablespoon (½ oz/15 g) butter

1 tablespoon chopped fresh basil

Arrange the fish in a single layer on a plate. Brush with a little of the oil. Season with salt, sprinkle with half the lemon juice and pepper to taste. Pour on the wine. Set aside to marinate for 1–2 hours, turning occasionally.

Prepare a fire in a charcoal grill or preheat a gas grill to high heat.

Drain the fish steaks, discarding the marinade. Place the fish on the grill rack and cook until just cooked through, 3–4 minutes on each side.

Meanwhile, heat the remaining oil and the butter in a saucepan over low heat; do not allow to brown. Turn off heat and add the remaining lemon juice and the basil. Add pepper to taste.

Arrange the fish on a serving dish, pour the oil and butter over and serve at once.

Serves 6

Sesame Salmon Steaks

¹⁄₃ cup (1 oz/30 g) sesame seeds

1 teaspoon salt

4 salmon steaks, about 1 inch (2.5 cm) thick, center bones removed

In a small saucepan or frying pan, toast the sesame seeds over low heat, stirring constantly, until golden and fragrant, about 4 minutes. Stir in the salt, then transfer seeds to a plate to cool.

Preheat a two-sided electric indoor grill or ridged grill pan according to the manufacturer's instructions.

Dip both sides of each salmon steak in the sesame seed mixture to coat.

If using the two-sided grill, place the fish on the grill, close the cover, and cook until the salmon is just cooked through, 4–5 minutes.

If using the grill pan, cook the salmon until it is just cooked through, 8–10 minutes, turning once midway through the cooking time.

Transfer the salmon to a serving dish and serve at once.

Serves 4

Garlic Shrimp

¼ cup (2 fl oz/60 ml) olive oil

4 large cloves garlic, very finely chopped

1 teaspoon red pepper flakes

2 tablespoons fresh lemon juice

2 tablespoons dry sherry

1 teaspoon paprika

1 lb (480 g) medium shrimp (prawns), peeled and deveined

Salt and ground black pepper

Chopped fresh flat-leaf (Italian) parsley, for garnish

Fresh crusty bread, to serve

Lemon wedges, to serve

In a small frying pan over medium heat, warm the oil. Add the garlic and red pepper flakes and sauté for 1 minute. Remove from heat and add the lemon juice, sherry and paprika. Pour about half of the mixture into a small bowl and set aside.

Prepare a fire in a charcoal grill or preheat a gas grill to medium-high heat.

Brush the shrimp with some of the remaining garlic–oil mixture, place on grill rack, and cook, turning once and brushing with more garlic–oil mixture, until shrimp turn pink and curl slightly, about 3 minutes in total.

Season to taste with salt and pepper. Sprinkle with reserved garlic–oil mixture and chopped parsley. Serve with fresh bread and lemon wedges.

Serves 4

233

Sea Perch with Herb Butter and Lemon

4 sea perch fillets

2 lemons

¼ cup (2 oz/60 g) butter

½ teaspoon salt

⅓ teaspoon ground black pepper

2 teaspoons finely chopped fresh flat-leaf (Italian) parsley

1 teaspoon chopped fresh dill

1 teaspoon chopped fresh chives

1 tablespoon very finely chopped red bell pepper

1 clove garlic, finely chopped

4 small zucchini (courgettes)

Cooked white rice, to serve

Dill sprigs, to serve (optional)

Prepare a fire in a charcoal grill or preheat a gas grill to medium-high heat.

Cut one lemon in halves and squeeze one half over the fish. Cut the remaining half into 2 wedges and the other lemon into 4 wedges; set aside.

Mash the butter with the salt, pepper, herbs, bell pepper and garlic. Spread evenly over the fish, place fish on the grill rack and cook until just cooked through, 3–4 minutes each side.

Slice each zucchini lengthwise without cutting through the stalk end. Drop into boiling, lightly salted water and simmer until just tender. Drain.

Arrange the fish and zucchini on serving plates with the cooked rice, lemon wedges and sprigs of dill, if liked. Spoon any sauce left in the pan evenly over the fish and serve at once.

NOTE If desired, the parsley and dill can be replaced with 2 teaspoons of chopped cilantro (fresh coriander).

Serves 4

Sea Scallops on Braised Fennel

FENNEL

2 bulbs fennel

2 tablespoons unsalted butter

½ cup (4 fl oz/120 ml) water

Salt and ground black pepper

¼ cup (1 oz/30 g) grated
Parmesan cheese

MARINADE AND
SCALLOPS

2 tablespoons olive oil

2 tablespoons fresh lemon juice

½ teaspoon salt

¼ teaspoon ground black pepper

1½ lb (720 g) shucked sea
scallops

To prepare the fennel, cut away the feathery tops from the fennel bulbs and trim the bottoms. Finely chop ¼ cup (⅓ oz/10 g) of the feathery fronds and set aside. Cut the fennel bulbs in half lengthwise and then cut lengthwise again into ¼-inch (5-mm) thick slices, leaving some of the core on each slice to hold it together.

In a 4-quart (4-l) casserole or Dutch oven, melt butter over medium heat. Add the fennel and stir until it starts to brown, 5–7 minutes. Add the water and salt and pepper to taste. Bring to a simmer, then reduce heat to low, cover and simmer, stirring

occasionally, until the fennel is very tender, about 20 minutes. Remove from the heat and stir in the cheese and 3 tablespoons of the reserved fennel fronds. Taste, add more salt and pepper, if needed, and keep warm.

For the scallops, in a small bowl, whisk together the olive oil, lemon juice, salt, pepper, and the remaining 1 tablespoon chopped fennel fronds. Add the scallops and toss to coat. Let marinate at room temperature, stirring occasionally, for 20–30 minutes.

Thread the marinated scallops onto skewers, leaving a little space between the pieces.

236

SEA SCALLOPS ON BRAISED FENNEL

Preheat a two-sided electric indoor grill or ridged grill pan according to the manufacturer's instructions.

If using the two-sided grill, place the skewers on the grill, close the cover, and cook, in batches as necessary, until the scallops are golden on the outside and opaque in the center, 3–4 minutes.

If using the grill pan, cook the skewers, in batches as necessary, until the scallops are golden on the outside and opaque in the center, 6–8 minutes, turning them once midway through the cooking time.

To serve, divide the fennel evenly among 4 plates and top with the scallop skewers.

Serves 4

Monkfish with Salsa Verde

½ cup (½ oz/15 g) packed fresh flat-leaf (Italian) parsley leaves

1 tablespoon drained capers

1 clove garlic

¼ teaspoon grated lemon zest

1 tablespoon fresh lemon juice

¼ cup (2 fl oz/60 ml) extra virgin olive oil, plus 1 tablespoon extra, for brushing

Salt and ground black pepper

1½ lb (720 g) monkfish, trimmed and cut crosswise into 8 pieces about 1 inch (2.5 cm) thick

Salt and ground black pepper

For the salsa, in the bowl of a food processor, combine the parsley, capers, garlic, lemon zest and lemon juice; pulse until chopped. Add oil and process until puréed, stopping once or twice to scrape down the sides of the bowl. Add salt and pepper to taste and set aside.

Preheat a two-sided electric indoor grill or ridged grill pan according to the manufacturer's instructions.

Brush both sides of the fish pieces with the extra oil and season with salt and pepper. If using the two-sided grill, place fish on grill, close the cover, and cook until the pieces are just cooked through, 1–1½ minutes.

If using the grill pan, cook until the fish pieces are just cooked through, about 3 minutes, turning once midway through the cooking time.

Divide the fish pieces among 4 plates and spoon some sauce over the top of each piece. Serve immediately.

Serves 4

Crab Cakes with Roasted Garlic Aïoli

AÏOLI

2 large heads garlic

1 tablespoon extra-virgin olive oil

1 cup (8 oz/240 g) mayonnaise (regular or reduced fat)

1 tablespoon fresh lemon juice, plus more as needed

Salt and ground black pepper

CRAB CAKES

1 large egg, lightly beaten

1/4 cup (2 oz/60 g) mayonnaise (regular or reduced fat)

1/4 cup (3 oz/90 g) minced red (Spanish) onion

1/4 cup (1/3 oz/10 g) chopped fresh flat-leaf (Italian) parsley

1/4 cup (1 oz/30 g) fine dry bread crumbs, plus 2/3 cup (3 oz/90 g) extra

1 tablespoon coarse-grain mustard

1/2 teaspoon Worcestershire sauce

1/4 teaspoon salt

1/4 teaspoon ground black pepper

1 lb (480 g) fresh lump crabmeat, picked over for bits of shell and cartilage

Preheat an oven to 325°F (165°C).

For the aïoli, remove the papery skin from the garlic heads. With a sharp knife, cut the top off the garlic, exposing the cloves. Place the garlic on a square of aluminum foil and drizzle with the olive oil. Bring the edges of the foil together and seal. Bake until the cloves are tender, 50–60 minutes. When cool enough to handle, slip the garlic cloves out of their skins.

In a blender or food processor, combine the garlic, mayonnaise and lemon juice; blend until smooth. Add salt and pepper to taste. The aïoli will keep, covered, in the refrigerator for up to 1 week.

For the crab cakes, in a bowl, combine the egg, mayonnaise, onion, parsley, the ¼ cup (1 oz/ 30 g) bread crumbs, mustard, Worcestershire sauce, salt and pepper. Stir the mixture until smooth. Add the crabmeat and mix gently. Form into eight ½-inch (12-mm) thick patties. Spread the remaining ⅔ cup (3 oz/90 g) bread crumbs in a shallow dish. Working with one crab cake at a time, dredge the crab cakes with the bread crumbs until coated on all sides.

Preheat a two-sided electric indoor grill or ridged grill pan

according to the manufacturer's instructions.

If using the two-sided grill, arrange crab cakes on the grill, close the cover, and cook until they are golden, 4–6 minutes.

If using the grill pan, cook crab cakes, in batches as necessary, until golden, 6–8 minutes, turning them carefully midway through the cooking time.

Divide the crab cakes among 4 plates and serve with the aïoli.

Serves 4

Spicy Fish Paste in Banana Leaf

2 lemongrass stalks, tender heart section only, chopped

6 candlenuts, soaked in water for 10 minutes, or blanched almonds

1 piece fresh ginger, ½ inch (1 cm) long, peeled

2 purple (Asian) shallots, cut into fourths

4 cloves garlic

8 fresh small red chili peppers, seeded and coarsely chopped

About 3 tablespoons water

2 teaspoons ground coriander

¼ teaspoon ground turmeric

2 tablespoons vegetable oil

¾ cup (6 fl oz/180 ml) coconut cream

1 teaspoon salt

1½ teaspoons sugar

Dash of ground white pepper

1½ lb (720 g) white fish fillets, preferably Spanish or king mackerel, cut into 1-inch (2.5-cm) dice

6 kaffir lime leaves, cut into very fine slivers, or shredded zest of 1 lime

24 pieces banana leaf, each 6 inches (15 cm) square

Leaves from 1 bunch basil

Fresh red chili pepper slivers

For the spice paste, in a blender, combine lemongrass, candlenuts or almonds, ginger, shallots, garlic and chilies. Blend to a smooth paste, adding water as needed to facilitate blending. Add the coriander and turmeric and blend to combine.

In a wok over medium heat, warm the vegetable oil. Add the spice paste and fry, stirring frequently, until fragrant and the oil takes on a red hue, about 3 minutes. Stir in the coconut cream, salt, sugar and white pepper; simmer until mixture forms a fragrant thick cream, 3–5 minutes. Remove from the heat and let cool.

Place fish in a food processor fitted with the metal blade and process to a smooth paste. Add the spice paste and half of the kaffir lime leaf slivers or lime zest and pulse just until the fish absorbs the spice paste.

Before forming the parcels, first soften the banana leaves. Bring a saucepan filled with water to a boil. Working with 1 piece of leaf at a time and using tongs, dip the leaf into the boiling water for a few seconds. Lift it out, drain well and place, shiny side down, on a work surface so that the grain runs horizontally to you. Place a few basil leaves in the midsection of the leaf.

Spread 3 tablespoons of the fish mixture down the middle (along the grain), forming a flat log about 1½ inches (4 cm) wide by 4 inches (10 cm) long. Scatter a few of the remaining lime leaf slivers or lime zest shreds and slivers of red chili on top. Fold the bottom and top edges over the filling, overlapping in the middle. Press down and flatten the ends; seal both ends with toothpicks to form flat parcels.

Repeat with the remaining leaves and filling. The parcels may be formed several hours in advance and refrigerated.

Prepare a fire in a charcoal grill. When the coals are ash white, position grill rack 3–4 inches (7.5–10 cm) from the coals and place the parcels on it. Grill, turning once, until the parcels feel firm when pressed, about 3 minutes per side.

Serve the parcels hot, warm or at room temperature. Remove the leaf before eating.

Serves 6

Salmon with Horseradish Potatoes

1 salmon fillet, skin on, about 1½ lb (750 g)

1 teaspoon salt

1 teaspoon cracked black pepper

4 large baking potatoes, about 14 oz (420 g) each

1 cup (8 fl oz/250 ml) heavy (double) cream

¼ cup (2 oz/60 g) unsalted butter

1 teaspoon salt

⅛ teaspoon ground white pepper

½ cup (4 oz/140 g) peeled and finely grated fresh horseradish

¼ cup (2 fl oz/60 ml) vegetable oil

3 tablespoons unsalted butter

1 teaspoon finely chopped golden (French) shallot

1 teaspoon chopped fresh flat-leaf (Italian) parsley, plus 4 sprigs extra

Juice of ½ lemon

Season the salmon on both sides with the salt. Spread the cracked pepper on a large plate and press the flesh side of the salmon into it until all the pepper adheres. Cut the fillet into 4 equal pieces and place on a platter. Cover with plastic wrap and refrigerate while making the potatoes.

For the potatoes, preheat an oven to 400°F (200°C). Prick the potatoes in several places with a fork, place on a baking sheet and bake until tender, 40–50 minutes.

While the potatoes are baking, make the horseradish cream. In a small saucepan over medium heat, combine cream, butter, salt and white pepper. Bring almost to a boil then remove from heat. Stir and let cool for 10 minutes. Transfer to a blender and add the grated horseradish. Process until smooth, about 30 seconds. Pour the horseradish cream into the original saucepan and let cool completely. Strain through a fine-mesh sieve into another saucepan.

When the potatoes are done, reheat the horseradish cream over medium-low heat. Remove the potatoes from the oven, but leave the oven on. Cut the potatoes in half and scoop out the pulp into a bowl. Add the

horseradish cream and, using an electric mixer, beat until completely smooth. Keep warm.

Prepare a fire in a charcoal grill or preheat a gas grill to medium–high heat. Brush the salmon pieces with some of the oil and place on the grill rack, flesh side down. Cook until golden brown and almost crisp, 3–4 minutes. Carefully turn the fish over and cook for 2–3 minutes more, until just cooked through.

In a small pan over medium heat, sauté the remaining olive oil, butter and shallot for 1 minute. Add the chopped parsley and lemon juice and heat through.

To serve, divide the potatoes among warmed individual plates, top each with a piece of fish, drizzle with some of the butter–oil mixture and garnish with the parsley sprigs.

Serves 4

VEGETABLES
AND SALADS

Eggplant and Goat Cheese Rolls

1 eggplant (aubergine)

Salt

Olive oil, for brushing

Ground black pepper

1/3 cup (1/2 oz/15 g) chopped fresh chives

3 cloves garlic, minced

Balsamic vinegar, for sprinkling

Leaves from 12 fresh thyme sprigs, finely chopped, or 1 tablespoon dried thyme, crumbled

1 log (7 oz/210 g) fresh goat cheese, at room temperature

Cut off and discard a thin slice from the stem and blossom ends of the eggplant. Cut the eggplant lengthwise into slices 1/4 inch (5 mm) thick. Lay the slices on a double thickness of paper towels and sprinkle generously with salt. Let stand until beads of water appear on the surface, about 20 minutes. Rinse with cold running water to remove the salt and bitter juices, then pat dry with extra paper towels.

Prepare a fire in a charcoal grill, or preheat a ridged grill pan until it is very hot. Brush the eggplant slices lightly on one side with olive oil, then place them on the grill in a single

layer, oiled sides down. Brush the tops with additional oil and grill until the eggplant begins to soften and the grill marks are clearly visible, then turn and continue grilling until soft but not too deeply browned, about 4 minutes total. As the eggplant slices are done, use tongs to transfer them to a large platter.

Arrange half of the slices in a single layer on another platter and sprinkle with salt and pepper to taste. Scatter half of the chives and half of the garlic evenly over the eggplant and sprinkle with a little balsamic vinegar. Sprinkle all the thyme evenly over the top. Top with the remaining eggplant slices in a single layer, then scatter the remaining chives and garlic over the top. Sprinkle with a little more balsamic vinegar. Let stand in a cool place for at least 2 hours, or cover and refrigerate for up to 3 days.

When ready to serve, carefully spread each eggplant slice with an equal amount of the goat cheese and roll up tightly. Secure with a toothpick, if necessary. Serve at room temperature.

Serves 4 to 6

Corn with Flavored Butters

8 ears corn, with husks

SWEET BUTTER

1 cup (8 oz/240 g) butter, softened

2 tablespoons grated orange zest

1/4 teaspoon ground nutmeg

1/4 teaspoon ground cinnamon

1/4 teaspoon ground cardamom

ZESTY CHEESE BUTTER

3 oz (90 g) butter, softened

1½ oz (45 g) shredded sharp Cheddar or Swiss cheese, or crumbled blue cheese

1 oz (30 g) finely chopped green (spring) onion

½ teaspoon white wine Worcestershire sauce, to taste

1/4 teaspoon chili powder

1/4 teaspoon black pepper

Pull down husks from corn, exposing kernels but leaving husk attached at bottom. Pull away silk. Rinse corn; rewrap corn with husks and tie securely in 2 or 3 places with kitchen string. Immerse cobs in cold water for 15–30 minutes, or until the strings and husks are thoroughly soaked (this prevents them from burning on the grill).

While corn is soaking, combine all ingredients for the butter of your choice in a medium mixing bowl; stir until well blended. Cover and set aside. (Or, prepare butter ahead and chill; before using, let stand at room temperature for 30 minutes to soften.)

Prepare a fire in a charcoal grill or preheat a gas grill to medium-high heat.

Remove corn from water, place on grill rack and cook, turning frequently, for 25–35 minutes for tender young corn and 40–50 minutes for more mature corn, or until kernels are tender. Remove strings and husks from corn. Serve corn with the flavored butter of your choice.

Serves 8

Filled Baked Potatoes

8 medium baking potatoes

AVOCADO FILLING

1 avocado, peeled and seeded

Juice of ½ lemon

2 green (spring) onions, chopped

Salt and black pepper, to taste

CHILI FILLING

2 tablespoons olive oil

1 small onion, chopped

1 clove garlic

1 can (10 oz/330 g) red kidney beans, drained and rinsed

2 teaspoons dried oregano

1 tablespoon ground cumin

½ teaspoon chili powder, or to taste

½ cup (4 fl oz/120 ml) ketchup (tomato sauce)

2 tablespoons tomato paste

2 teaspoons Worcestershire sauce

PESTO AND CHEESE FILLING

½ cup (4 fl oz/120 ml) pesto

2 bocconcini (mozzarella balls), chopped

GORGONZOLA AND PISTACHIO FILLING

6 oz (180 g) Gorgonzola or other blue cheese

⅓ cup (2½ fl oz/80 ml) light (single) cream

½ cup (2 oz/60 g) pistachio nuts, shelled

Prepare a fire in a charcoal grill or preheat a gas grill to high heat.

Scrub potatoes and pierce with a fork. Wrap each potato in aluminum foil, place on grill rack or directly on hot coals, and cook for about 45 minutes, or until tender when pierced with a fork. Remove from the heat, slash a cross in the tops, and, holding with a tea towel to avoid being burnt, squeeze each potato gently to open it up. Top with your choice of filling(s).

While potatoes are cooking, prepare filling(s). For avocado filling, chop the avocado flesh then combine with all remaining ingredients.

For chili filling, heat the oil in a pan. Add onion and garlic and cook, stirring, on low heat for 2 minutes. Add all remaining ingredients and cook, stirring occasionally, for 5 minutes.

For pesto and cheese filling, combine pesto and bocconcini.

For Gorgonzola and pistachio filling, process cheese in a food processor for 20 seconds. With motor running, pour in cream in a steady stream and process until combined. Pile onto the baked potatoes and sprinkle with pistachios.

Serves 8

Lentil Patties with Onions and Aïoli

LENTIL PATTIES

4½ oz (135 g) green or brown lentils

1 egg

¾ oz (20 g) toasted wheat germ

1 oz (30 g) fine dry bread crumbs

2 tablespoons tahini (sesame seed paste)

2 cloves garlic, crushed

½ teaspoon salt

3 tablespoons olive oil

1 large red (Spanish) onion, sliced

AÏOLI

6 cloves garlic, or to taste

1 cup (8 fl oz/240 ml) olive oil

Salt and ground black pepper

Salad leaves, to garnish

8 cherry tomatoes, cut in halves, to serve

For patties, rinse lentils and drain. Place in a saucepan with water to cover and bring to the boil. Reduce heat, cover, and simmer for 30 minutes, or until tender. Drain lentils well.

In a blender or food processor, blend or process lentils and egg until nearly smooth. Transfer mixture to a medium mixing bowl. Add wheat germ, bread crumbs, tahini, garlic and salt; stir well. Shape the mixture into 4 patties, each about ½ inch (1 cm) thick.

Heat 1 tablespoon oil in a large frying pan. Cook the onion for 3–5 minutes, or until tender. Remove, cover and keep warm.

Add the remaining oil to the pan and cook patties, turning once, for 5–7 minutes, or until golden brown all over.

Meanwhile, for aïoli, mash the garlic until smooth and place in a mixing bowl or the bowl of a food processor. Slowly add the oil, whisking briskly or processing to make a smooth, thick emulsion. Add salt and pepper to taste. Top each patty with onion, aïoli and salad leaves and serve with tomatoes.

Serves 4

Squash with Brown Sugar Glaze

3 acorn squash or small pumpkins, about 1 lb (480 g) each, halved, seeds removed

1 tablespoon cooking oil

2 oz (60 g) raisins (optional)

2½ oz (75 g) packed brown sugar

Pinch of ground nutmeg

2 tablespoons butter

2 tablespoons granola or chopped nuts of your choice

Prepare a fire in a charcoal grill or preheat a gas grill to medium-high heat.

Place each pumpkin half, cut-side up, on a piece of heavy foil. Brush cut sides of halves with oil. Sprinkle raisins over halves, if using. Bring edges of foil together; seal to form parcels. Cook on an uncovered grill for 40–50 minutes, or until squash or pumpkins are tender when pierced with a fork.

Combine brown sugar and nutmeg. Unwrap squash or pumpkins on the grill. Sprinkle with brown sugar–nutmeg mixture and dot with butter.

Carefully rewrap and grill for about 5 minutes more, or until brown sugar and butter melt. Sprinkle with granola or nuts and serve hot.

Serves 6

Grilled Polenta with Tomato Sauce

POLENTA

4 cups (32 fl oz/960 ml) water

½ teaspoon salt

1 cup (6 oz/180 g) polenta or coarse yellow cornmeal (maize flour)

3 oz (90 g) grated Romano or Parmesan cheese

TOMATO SAUCE

6 medium-size ripe tomatoes

1 tablespoon olive oil

2 green (spring) onions, sliced

2 cloves garlic, crushed

¼ teaspoon salt

¼ teaspoon pepper

¼ cup (2 fl oz/60 ml) olive oil

1 tablespoon finely chopped fresh basil

1 tablespoon finely chopped fresh sage or thyme or 1 teaspoon dried sage or thyme, crushed

Parmesan cheese, shredded

Hot cooked asparagus, to serve

Prepare polenta the day before. In a medium saucepan, bring 3 cups (32 fl oz/750 ml) of the water to the boil. Add the salt. Combine polenta or cornmeal with the remaining water in a small bowl; add grated cheese. Slowly add the polenta mixture to the boiling water, stirring constantly. Cook, stirring, until the mixture returns to the boil.

Reduce heat to very low. Cover and simmer, stirring from time to time, for 30–40 minutes, or until very thick. Pour the hot mixture into a greased 8- x 4- x 2-inch (20- x 10- x 5-cm) loaf tin. Cool for 1 hour. Cover and chill for several hours or overnight, until firm.

On the day of serving, to make the sauce, grill or broil the tomatoes, turning occasionally, for 5–6 minutes, or until skin is blistered and charred in spots. Remove from heat; cool slightly, then halve tomatoes. Squeeze out seeds; do not peel. Chop flesh. In a large frying pan, heat the oil and and cook the green onion and garlic for 2 minutes.

Stir in tomato, salt and pepper. Bring to boil; reduce heat and simmer, covered, for 5 minutes.

In a small bowl, combine the ¼ cup oil and the herbs. Cut the chilled polenta into 16 slices, each about ½ inch (1 cm) thick. Brush both sides with herbed oil. Grill or broil the polenta slices for 6–7 minutes, or until bottoms are golden brown. Brush tops with herbed oil, turn and cook for 6–7 minutes more, or until golden brown.

Arrange the polenta on serving plates; spoon sauce over the top. Top with shredded Parmesan and asparagus.

Serves 8

Tricolor Coleslaw

3 tablespoons cider vinegar

1 tablespoon sugar

2 cups (16 fl oz/480 ml) mayonnaise

¼ teaspoon salt

¼ teaspoon ground black pepper

3 tablespoons finely chopped fresh flat-leaf (Italian) parsley

½ small head red cabbage, shredded (about 3 cups/9 oz/270 g)

1 small head green cabbage, shredded (about 5 cups/15 oz/450 g)

2 carrots, peeled and shredded (about 1 cup/5 oz/150 g)

In a large serving bowl, combine the vinegar, sugar, mayonnaise, salt, pepper and parsley. Stir well.

Add the cabbages and carrot to the dressing and, using tongs, toss to coat all vegetables evenly.

Cover with plastic wrap and chill for at least 2 hours or for up to 8 hours before serving.

Serves 6 to 8

Greek Salad

½ cup (4 fl oz/120 ml) virgin olive oil

2–3 tablespoons fresh lemon juice

3 tablespoons dried oregano

Cracked black pepper

1 clove garlic, very finely chopped (optional)

2–3 cups (2–3 oz/60–90 g) torn assorted salad greens, such as arugula (rocket), romaine (cos) lettuce, escarole (Batavian endive) or frisée

4 small ripe tomatoes, cored and cut into wedges

1 large cucumber, peeled, seeded and cut into wedges

1 red (Spanish) onion, thinly sliced into rings

2 small green bell peppers (capsicums), seeded, deribbed and thinly sliced crosswise into rings

½ lb (250 g) feta cheese, coarsely crumbled

20 Kalamata olives

For the dressing, in a bowl, stir together the oil, lemon juice, oregano, pepper to taste, and the garlic, if using. Set aside.

In a large salad bowl, combine the greens, tomato, cucumber, onion and bell pepper. Drizzle the dressing over the top and toss gently to mix. Sprinkle the feta cheese and olives over the top and serve immediately.

Serves 4

Tomato, Mozzarella and Basil Salad

12 oz (360 g) fresh mozzarella cheese, drained

1/4 cup (2 fl oz/60 ml) extra virgin olive oil

Salt and ground black pepper

12 fresh basil leaves, thinly sliced

2 tablespoons coarsely chopped fresh flat-leaf (Italian) parsley

12 oz (360 g) round and/or pear-shaped cherry tomatoes, in a mixture of colors

1/4 cup (1 1/2 oz/45 g) large black olives, such as Kalamata

If using large balls of mozzarella, cut them into 1/2-inch (1-cm) dice. If using smaller balls, cut them into quarters.

In a bowl, toss the mozzarella with 2 tablespoons of the olive oil and salt and pepper to taste. Add half of the basil and half of the parsley. Toss gently.

If using round cherry tomatoes, cut them in halves. If using pear-shaped tomatoes, leave them whole. In another bowl, combine the tomatoes with the remaining 2 tablespoons olive oil, salt and pepper to taste, and the remaining basil and parsley. Toss gently.

Mound the mozzarella in the center of individual plates. Make a ring of the seasoned tomatoes around the edge and garnish with the olives. Serve at once.

Serves 4 to 6

Niçoise Salad with Tuna

12 tiny new potatoes

8 oz (240 g) green beans, ends removed

1 bunch curly endive (chicory), washed and dried

3 hard-cooked (hard-boiled) eggs, peeled and cut in halves

8 oz (240 g) cherry tomatoes

12 small black olives

2 cans tuna (each 7 oz/210 g), drained

1 tablespoon olive oil

3 green (spring) onions, finely chopped

1 tablespoon lemon juice

Salt and ground black pepper

DRESSING

⅓ cup (3 fl oz/90 ml) red wine vinegar

2 anchovy fillets

2 teaspoons Dijon mustard

Ground pepper, to taste

⅔ cup (5 fl oz/150 ml) extra-virgin olive oil

Place potatoes in a saucepan. Cover with cold water, bring to a boil, then simmer over medium heat for 10–12 minutes, or until tender. Drain.

Cook beans in boiling salted water for about 4 minutes, or just until tender. Arrange the potatoes, beans, endive, eggs, tomatoes and olives on a large platter. Combine the tuna with the oil, green onions, lemon juice, salt and pepper. Arrange on the platter.

For the dressing, combine the vinegar, anchovy fillets, mustard and pepper in a small bowl and whisk until combined. Add the oil gradually, whisking until thoroughly blended. Pour dressing over salad ingredients and serve at once.

Serves 6

Grilled Vegetable Couscous

1 fennel bulb, trimmed and thinly sliced

1 red bell pepper (capsicum), cored, deseeded and cut into fourths

2 small zucchini (courgettes), trimmed and cut lengthwise into ¼-inch (5-mm) thick slices

3 large field mushrooms

¼ cup (2 fl oz/60 ml) olive oil, plus 3 tablespoons extra

Salt and ground black pepper

1 cup (3 oz/90 g) uncooked instant couscous

1 teaspoon grated lemon zest

1 tablespoon fresh lemon juice

2 green (spring) onions, thinly sliced

¼ cup (⅓ oz/10 g) chopped fresh flat-leaf (Italian) parsley

Preheat a two-sided electric indoor grill or ridged grill pan according to the manufacturer's instructions.

In a large, shallow baking dish or roasting pan, place the vegetables (keeping the different types of vegetable as separate as possible). Toss them with the ¼ cup (2 fl oz/60 ml) of olive oil and season with salt and pepper to taste.

If using the two-sided grill, place vegetables on grill in a single layer, close cover and cook, in batches as necessary, until browned and tender, 3–5 minutes (the zucchini and mushrooms will take less time than the fennel and peppers).

If using the grill pan, cook the vegetables, in batches as necessary, until browned and tender, 6–10 minutes (the zucchini and mushrooms will take less time than the fennel and pepper). Turn vegetables midway through cooking time.

Transfer the vegetables to a cutting board.

Meanwhile, cook the couscous according to package directions. Keep it covered so it will stay warm while you finish preparing the vegetables.

Cut the grilled vegetables into 1- to 1½-inch (2.5–4 cm) pieces. Transfer the couscous to a large bowl and fluff with a fork. Toss the couscous with the remaining olive oil, salt and pepper to taste, the lemon zest and lemon juice. Add the cut-up vegetables, green onions and parsley and toss gently. Serve warm or at room temperature.

Serves 4

Roasted Tomato Salad

1¾ lb (840 g) large ripe tomatoes

1 bunch green (spring) onions, cut in halves

6 cloves garlic, peeled and cut in halves

¼ cup (2 fl oz/60 ml) extra virgin olive oil

1 tablespoon fresh thyme leaves

Ground black pepper

1 tablespoon balsamic vinegar

1 tablespoon finely chopped fresh flat-leaf (Italian) parsley

Peel the tomatoes by covering with boiling water for about 30 seconds then plunging them into cold water. Drain, then peel off the skins. Halve tomatoes and squeeze out seeds. Drain for 30 minutes on a wire rack.

Preheat oven to 375°F (190°C/ Gas Mark 5). Arrange tomatoes, cut sides up, in a baking dish. Add the green onions and garlic. Pour on the oil and scatter with thyme and black pepper. Bake, uncovered, for 30 minutes. Remove from oven and, when cool enough to handle, arrange tomatoes, cut sides down, on a serving plate. Spoon over the green onions and garlic.

Whisk the vinegar into the oil that remains in the baking dish. Drizzle the mixture over the tomatoes and onions.

Sprinkle with the parsley and serve warm or at room temperature. This salad makes a good accompaniment to grilled or roasted meats.

Serves 4 to 6

Potato Salad with Red Wine Vinegar

8 medium boiling potatoes, peeled and cubed

¼ cup (2 fl oz/60 ml) red wine vinegar

2 tablespoons chopped dill

2 small red (Spanish) onions, sliced

⅓ cup (3 fl oz/90 ml) sour cream

⅓ cup (3 fl oz/90 ml) mayonnaise

Salt and ground black pepper

Place the potatoes in a large saucepan, add water to cover and bring to a boil over low heat. Cook until tender. Drain.

Gently toss the potatoes with the vinegar, dill and onions.

Combine the sour cream and mayonnaise. Add salt and pepper to taste. Gently fold into the potatoes and serve warm or at room temperature.

Serves 6

Wild Rice Salad

1 cup (6 oz/180 g) wild rice

½ cup (3 oz/90 g) long-grain white rice

2 stalks celery, chopped

1 onion, chopped

1 apple, peeled and chopped

1 red bell pepper (capsicum), chopped

½ cup (4 fl oz/120 ml) mayonnaise

2 teaspoons Dijon mustard

1 clove garlic, crushed

¼ cup (2 fl oz/60 ml) olive or safflower oil

2 tablespoons tarragon vinegar

Cook the wild rice and white rice separately in boiling water until just tender, about 30 minutes for wild rice and 15 minutes for white rice. Drain and let cool.

Place the rice in a serving bowl with the celery, onion, apple and bell pepper. Mix well. Combine the remaining ingredients, pour over the salad and mix well.

Serves 6

Tomato and Pesto Pasta Salad

1 cup (1 oz/30 g) loosely packed basil leaves

¼ cup (1½ oz/45 g) pine nuts, toasted

1 clove garlic, peeled

¾ cup (6 fl oz/180 ml) olive oil

12 oz (360 g) penne

¾ cup (4 oz/120 g) sun-dried tomatoes

5 oz (150 g) feta cheese or bocconcini (mozzarella balls), cut into chunks

½ cup (3 oz/90 g) black olives, pitted

⅓ cup (1½ oz/45 g) grated Parmesan (optional)

Process basil leaves in a food processor with the pine nuts and garlic until very finely chopped. With motor running, gradually add oil; process until puréed.

Cook pasta in boiling salted water until al dente. Drain, refresh under cold water and toss in a little oil to prevent pasta sticking together.

Place pasta in a serving bowl with the tomatoes, cheese and olives. Mix in the basil dressing and top with Parmesan, if using.

Serves 6

Grilled Tofu, Tomato and Olive Salad

TOFU AND MARINADE

15 oz (450 g) package extra-firm tofu, drained

½ cup (4 fl oz/120 ml) fresh lemon juice

⅓ cup (3 fl oz/90 ml) olive oil

3 large cloves garlic, minced

1 teaspoon dried rosemary, crumbled

Salt and ground black pepper

SALAD

1 ripe tomato, diced

½ cup (2½ oz/75 g) coarsely chopped black olives

1 clove garlic, minced

1 teaspoon grated lemon zest

1 tablespoon olive oil

¾ cup (1½ oz/45 g) coarsely chopped watercress or arugula (rocket)

To prepare the tofu, line a baking sheet with plastic wrap. Cut the tofu in half crosswise, then cut each piece in half horizontally and place on the baking sheet. Cover the tofu with another sheet of plastic wrap. Top this with another baking sheet, then weight the top sheet with a heavy object. Refrigerate for 45 minutes to press out the excess moisture from the tofu.

In a glass dish, combine lemon juice, olive oil, garlic, rosemary and salt and pepper to taste. Uncover the baking sheets and pour off the liquid from the tofu. Place tofu in the marinade and turn pieces to coat. Cover the dish and marinate the tofu for 1–2 hours, turning it once.

For the salad, in a bowl, combine the tomato, olives, garlic, lemon zest and oil. Set aside.

Preheat a two-sided electric indoor grill or ridged grill pan according to the manufacturer's instructions.

Remove tofu from marinade, shaking off excess. Discard the marinade.

If using the two-sided grill, arrange tofu on grill, close the cover, and cook until it is nicely browned, 2½–3 minutes.

If using the grill pan, cook the tofu until it is nicely browned, about 6 minutes, turning once midway through cooking time.

Divide the tofu among 4 plates. Toss the watercress or arugula with the tomato mixture and add salt and pepper to taste. Spoon the salad over the tofu and serve immediately.

Serves 4

Couscous Tabbouleh

1½ cups (8 oz/240 g) instant couscous

1 cup (8 fl oz/240 ml) boiling water

⅓ cup (2½ fl oz/75 ml) fresh lemon juice

2 tablespoons olive oil

1 teaspoon salt

3 large tomatoes, peeled, seeded and finely chopped

½ cup (1¾ oz/50 g) finely sliced green (spring) onions

¼ cup (¼ oz/7 g) finely chopped fresh mint leaves

1 cup (1 oz/60 g) finely chopped fresh flat-leaf (Italian) parsley

Place the couscous in a large bowl. Pour on the boiling water and stir thoroughly. Cover and set aside to allow the couscous to absorb the water and swell.

For the dressing, in a small bowl, combine the lemon juice, olive oil and salt; whisk well.

In a large serving bowl, combine the tomato, green onion, mint and parsley. Stir the couscous with a fork to separate the grains and break up any lumps. Add the couscous to the serving bowl and mix all of the ingredients thoroughly. Pour on the dressing and mix again thoroughly. Serve at room temperature or chilled.

Serves 6

Antipasto Salad Platter

½ cup (4 fl oz/120 ml) olive oil

2 tablespoons red wine vinegar

1 clove garlic, crushed

1 tablespoon finely chopped fresh flat-leaf (Italian) parsley

1 tablespoon finely chopped capers

1 tablespoon finely chopped anchovy fillets

1 teaspoon tomato paste

½ teaspoon sugar

Ground black pepper

1 eggplant (aubergine), about 2 lb (980 g), sliced into ½-inch (1-cm) rounds

Salt

2 red bell peppers (capsicums)

1 yellow bell pepper (capsicum)

½ cup (2 oz/60 g) all-purpose (plain) flour

Olive oil, for frying

4 plum (Roma) tomatoes, sliced lengthwise

10 oz (300 g) bocconcini (mozzarella balls), sliced

For the dressing, in a bowl, combine the oil, vinegar, garlic, parsley, capers, anchovy, tomato paste, sugar and pepper to taste. Whisk together thoroughly.

Place the eggplant slices in a colander. Lightly sprinkle with salt and set aside for 30 minutes.

Prepare a fire in a charcoal grill, preheat a gas grill to medium-high heat or preheat a broiler (griller).

Halve the bell peppers; remove the seeds and membrane. Place the bell pepper halves on the grill rack or under the broiler and cook until the skins are blackened. Place the halves in a plastic bag and let cool. When cold enough to handle, peel off skins and slice flesh thinly.

Rinse eggplant slices and drain on kitchen paper. Dust slices lightly with flour. In a large frying pan, heat enough oil to fry the slices, in batches, until golden on both sides. As each slice is cooked, dip it in the prepared dressing and arrange around the serving platter.

Cook the tomato slices for a few seconds on each side in the same pan as the eggplant. Place the tomato slices on top of the eggplant. Top the tomato with the bocconcini slices, then spoon a little dressing over each bocconcini slice. Arrange the bell pepper slices in the center of the serving platter. Spoon on the remaining dressing. Let stand at room temperature for at least 1 hour before serving.

Serves 6 to 8

DESSERTS

Lemon Meringue Pie

1 purchased or home-made 9-inch (23-cm) pastry case, baked blind and cooled

FILLING

1 cup (8 oz/240 g) sugar

⅓ cup (1½ oz/45 g) cornstarch (cornflour)

¼ teaspoon salt

2 cups (16 fl oz/480 ml) water

4 egg yolks, well beaten

3 tablespoons unsalted butter

½ cup (4 fl oz/120 ml) strained fresh lemon juice

Finely grated zest of 1 large lemon

MERINGUE

5 egg whites

¼ teaspoon cream of tartar

⅛ teaspoon salt

½ cup (4 oz/120 g) sugar

Preheat an oven to 350°F (180°C/Gas Mark 4).

For the filling, in a heavy non-aluminum saucepan, combine the sugar, cornstarch and salt and whisk until smooth. Stir in the water, a few drops at a time at first and then in greater amounts, adding more water gradually until the mixture is smooth. Stir in the egg yolks, whisking well to combine.

Place the saucepan over medium heat and bring to a boil, stirring constantly with a wooden spoon over the bottom and to the edge of the pan. Switch to a whisk occasionally to prevent lumps from forming.

When mixture reaches a boil, 7–8 minutes, boil for 1 minute, stirring constantly. Remove pan from heat, add the butter and gradually stir in the lemon juice, only a few drops at a time at first, until incorporated and the butter is melted. Stir in the lemon zest. Pour the hot filling into the cooled pie crust, then make the meringue immediately.

For the meringue, in a large, clean bowl, using an electric mixer on medium speed, beat the egg whites for a few seconds to break them up.

Add the cream of tartar and salt and continue beating until soft peaks form, about 2 minutes.

Increase the speed to high and add the sugar in a slow, steady stream, stopping occasionally to scrape down the sides of the bowl. Continue beating until stiff peaks form, 2–3 minutes.

Spoon about one-fourth of the meringue onto the top of the hot filling and spread it to meet the crust. Place the remaining meringue in the center of the pie and, using the back of a spoon, shape and spread the meringue into peaks. Bake until meringue is golden brown and firm to the touch, rotating a few times to promote even coloring, about 15 minutes. Transfer to a wire rack and let cool completely.

Serve at room temperature or store in the refrigerator for up to 1 day, uncovered. Bring to room temperature before serving.

Serves 6 to 8

Caramelized Fruit

2 firm, ripe peaches

2 firm, ripe plums

2 firm, ripe apricots

2 fresh figs

2 bananas

2 slices pineapple

Brown sugar

Ice cream, thick cream or natural (plain) yogurt, to serve

Honey and/or cinnamon (optional)

Prepare a fire in a charcoal grill or preheat a gas grill to medium-high heat.

Peel the stone fruit and cut in halves. Cut the figs in halves. Peel the bananas and cut each crosswise into four pieces. Cut each pineapple slice into four.

Arrange the fruit on a clean, hot grill plate and cook until browned with nice grill marks on one side. Sprinkle with the brown sugar, turn the fruit, and cook until the sugar bubbles and caramelizes.

Transfer to a large platter or individual serving dishes and serve with ice cream, thick cream or yogurt. If you wish, stir a little honey through the yogurt and spice it with a dash of ground cinnamon.

Serves 8

Mile-High Chocolate Cake

CAKE

2¼ cups (11½ oz/345 g) all-purpose (plain) flour

1½ teaspoons baking soda (bicarbonate of soda)

1 teaspoon salt

1¼ teaspoons baking powder

4 oz (120 g) unsweetened (bitter) chocolate, chopped

¾ cup (6 oz/180 g) unsalted butter, at room temperature

1¾ cups (14 oz/420 g) sugar

3 eggs

1 teaspoon vanilla extract (essence)

¾ cup (6 fl oz/180 ml) milk

FROSTING

2 cups (16 fl oz/480 ml) heavy (double) cream

15 oz (450 g) semisweet (plain) chocolate, chopped

⅓ cup (3 oz/90 g) unsalted butter, at room temperature

1½ tablespoons vanilla extract (essence)

Preheat an oven to 350°F (180°C/Gas Mark 4). Butter and line three 9-inch (23-cm) round cake pans.

For the cake, in a large bowl, mix together the flour, baking soda, salt and baking powder.

In the top pan of a double boiler or in a heatproof bowl set over (not touching) simmering water in a pan, melt the chocolate, stirring until smooth. Remove from the heat and let cool to room temperature.

In a large bowl, using an electric mixer on medium speed, beat the butter and sugar until light and fluffy, 3–5 minutes. Add the eggs, one at a time, beating well

after each addition. Then add the cooled chocolate and the vanilla and mix until blended.

Reduce speed to low and beat in flour mixture in three batches, alternating with the milk and beginning and ending with flour.

Divide batter evenly among the prepared pans. Bake until a wooden skewer inserted in the center of each cake comes out clean, 25–30 minutes. Transfer to racks and let cool in the pans for 15 minutes, then invert the cakes onto the racks to cool.

Meanwhile, for the frosting, in a heavy saucepan over high heat, bring the cream to a boil.

Remove from heat and add the chocolate, butter and vanilla, stirring constantly until both the chocolate and butter are melted and the mixture is smooth.

Place the pan in the refrigerator and stir every 15 minutes. The frosting will begin to set after about 50 minutes. Check every 5 minutes near this point for a spreadable consistency. (If the frosting becomes too thick, let it stand at room temperature, stirring occasionally, until it softens and becomes spreadable.)

To frost the cakes, place 1 cake layer, flat side up, on a 12-inch (30-cm) cake plate. Spread the top with one-fourth of the

frosting. Place the second cake layer, flat side up, on top of the first and flatten gently with your hand. Spread the top of the second layer with one-third of the remaining frosting. Place the third layer, flat side up, on top and again flatten gently.

Frost the top and sides of the cake quickly, using all of the remaining frosting. Using a flat-edged knife or icing spatula, make quick movements to create swirls on the top and sides of the cake. Let stand for about 1 hour to set the frosting, then serve at room temperature.

Serves 10 to 12

Strawberry Cheesecake

CRUST

1½ cups (4½ oz/135 g) graham cracker (sweet wholemeal biscuit) crumbs

2 tablespoons sugar

⅓ cup (3 oz/90 g) unsalted butter, melted

FILLING

3 cups (24 oz/720 g) cream cheese, at room temperature

1¼ cups (10 oz/300 g) sugar

6 eggs, at room temperature

2 cups (16 fl oz/480 ml) sour cream, at room temperature

⅓ cup (2 oz/60 g) all-purpose (plain) flour, sifted

2 teaspoons vanilla extract (essence)

Finely grated zest (rind) and juice of 1 lemon

½ cup (5 oz/150 g) strawberry jam

½ cup (2 oz/60 g) finely chopped, hulled strawberries

12 whole strawberries, hulled

Preheat oven to 350°F (180°C/ Gas Mark 4). Butter a spring-form pan 9½ inches (24 cm) in diameter and 3 inches (7.5 cm) deep.

For the crust, in a medium bowl, combine the crumbs, sugar and melted butter, breaking up any large crumbs and mixing well. Firmly press the mixture evenly over the bottom and 2 inches (5 cm) up the sides of the pan.

For the filling, in a large bowl, break the cream cheese into pieces. Using an electric mixer on medium speed, beat until soft and creamy, 2–3 minutes.

Add the sugar and beat until the mixture is smooth, 1–2 minutes. Add the eggs, one at a time, beating well after each addition. Reduce the speed to low and beat in the sour cream, flour, vanilla and lemon zest and juice until thoroughly blended.

Remove 1 cup (8 fl oz/240 ml) of the batter and place it in a small bowl. Add the strawberry jam, mixing thoroughly, and then gently mix in the chopped strawberries. Pour this mixture into the rest of the batter and stir just until incorporated. Pour into the prepared pan and jiggle the pan until the batter is level.

Bake for 1 hour. Turn off the heat and allow the cheesecake to rest undisturbed in the oven until set firm, about 30 minutes longer. Transfer to a rack and allow to cool. Cover and chill overnight before serving.

Just before serving, run a sharp knife around the pan sides to loosen the cake. Release the pan sides and place the cake on a plate. Arrange the whole strawberries evenly around the top.

Serves 12

Summer Berry Puddings

PUDDINGS

16 slices stale white bread, crusts removed

1/2 cup (4 oz/120 g) blueberries

1/2 cup (4 oz/120 g) raspberries

1/3 cup (3 oz/90 g) sugar

1/2 cup (4 oz/120 g) strawberries, chopped

Whipped cream and extra berries (optional), to serve

STRAWBERRY SAUCE

1 cup (8 oz/240 g) strawberries

3 tablespoons sugar

1 tablespoon water

For the puddings, line four 6-oz (9-cm) round molds or ramekins with bread, making sure there is no space between the pieces. Cut a "lid" for each from some of the bread.

Place blueberries and raspberries in a saucepan with the 1/3 cup (3 oz/90 g) sugar and cook on low heat, 3–4 minutes, stirring gently. Then add the chopped strawberries and cook for 1 minute longer.

Pour the fruit into the prepared molds and place a lid over each. Cover with plastic wrap and set a weight on the top of each pudding. Refrigerate overnight.

For the strawberry sauce, place the whole strawberries into a saucepan with the 3 tablespoons sugar and the water. Cook over low heat to dissolve the sugar.

Bring to a boil and simmer for 3 minutes or until strawberries are completely soft. Place in a food processor and purée. Strain through a fine sieve. Discard the contents of the sieve.

Unmold the puddings and drizzle with the strawberry sauce. Serve with whipped cream and berries, if desired.

Serves 4

Wild Berry and Apricot Trifle

6 oz (180 g) strawberry or raspberry jello (jelly) crystals

2 small purchased or home-made sponge or madeira cakes

1¼ cups (13 fl oz/390 ml) strawberry jam

1½ cups (12 fl oz/375 ml) sweet sherry

1 cup (8 oz/240 g) strawberries, hulled and halved

2 cups (16 oz/480 g) blueberries

2 cups (16 oz/480 g) raspberries

8 oz (240 g) fresh apricot halves

4 cups (32 fl oz/960 ml) milk

½ cup cornstarch (cornflour)

⅔ cup (5 oz/150 g) sugar

Pinch of salt

6 eggs, lightly beaten

2 teaspoons vanilla extract (essence)

Whipped cream, for decoration

Make up the jello according to directions on packet. Refrigerate until set, then chop roughly.

Cut cake into slices, spread with jam, sprinkle with sherry and set aside. Place berries and apricots in a bowl and toss gently until combined.

In a saucepan, scald 3 cups (24 fl oz/720 ml) of the milk. Mix the remaining milk with the cornstarch. When the milk is hot, add sugar and salt and stir until dissolved. Add cornstarch mixture and stir well. Cook custard over low heat, stirring constantly, until mixture boils and thickens. Add some of custard to the beaten eggs to warm them. Add egg mixture to custard and cook, stirring, for 3 minutes, or until the eggs are cooked and the custard coats a spoon. Pour custard into bowl, whisk in vanilla. Place a sheet of plastic on custard to prevent skin forming, then chill.

To assemble trifle, arrange half the cake slices over the base of a very large serving dish (or two large dishes), top with half the custard, then half the jello and half the berries and apricots. Repeat these layers, finishing with a layer of fruit. Refrigerate overnight. Just before serving, decorate with whipped cream.

NOTE This dessert is best made 1 day in advance.

Serves 20

Tiramisu

5 eggs, separated

¼ cup (2 oz/60 g) sugar

2 cups (1 lb/480 g) mascarpone cheese

¼ cup (2 fl oz/60 ml) dark rum

1 cup (8 fl oz/240 ml) very strong black coffee

24 sponge finger cookies (savoiardi/ladyfingers)

2 oz (60 g) grated milk chocolate or unsweetened cocoa powder

In a bowl, whisk the egg yolks and sugar until pale and thick. Fold in mascarpone and rum.

With an electric mixer on medium to high speed, beat the egg whites until soft peaks form. Stir one-third of the egg whites into the mascarpone mixture. Gently fold in the remaining egg whites.

Pour the coffee into a bowl. Dip each sponge finger cookie into the coffee for 1–2 seconds. Line the base of a large serving dish, or individual glasses, with half of the sponge finger cookies. Gently spread the mascarpone mixture over the sponge fingers.

Sprinkle with half of the grated chocolate or cocoa. Repeat with the remaining coffee, sponge finger cookies, mascarpone and chocolate or cocoa. Refrigerate overnight and serve chilled.

Serves 6 to 8

Cappuccino Gelato

1½ cups (12 fl oz/360 ml) milk

½ cup (4 fl oz/120 ml) light (single) cream

¼ cup (2 oz/60 g) sugar

4 extra-large egg yolks

2 teaspoons vanilla extract (essence)

2 tablespoons instant coffee granules dissolved in 1 tablespoon milk, or 3 tablespoons brewed coffee mixed with 1 tablespoon coffee liqueur

In a saucepan over medium heat, combine the milk, cream and sugar and stir to dissolve the sugar. Bring almost to a boil, then remove from the heat.

In a small bowl, stir together the egg yolks until blended.

Stir a few tablespoons of the hot milk mixture into the egg yolks. Then slowly pour the egg yolks into the remaining hot milk mixture, stirring constantly.

Place over low heat and cook, stirring, until thickened, about 2 minutes. Do not allow to boil. Immediately pour the mixture through a fine-mesh sieve into a bowl to remove any lumps.

Stir in the vanilla and the coffee mixture. Let cool, cover and chill well, at least 2 hours.

Transfer the coffee mixture to an ice-cream maker. Freeze according to the manufacturer's instructions.

Serves 4

Chocolate Hazelnut Cream Pavlova

MERINGUE

8 egg whites, at room temperature

1½ cups (12 oz/360 g) sugar

CHOCOLATE HAZELNUT CREAM

1¼ cups (10 fl oz/300 ml) heavy (double) cream, whipped

1 cup (4 oz/120 g) ground hazelnuts

4 oz (120 g) semisweet (plain) chocolate, melted and cooled

¼ cup (1 oz/30 g) chopped hazelnuts

Preheat an oven to 250°F (120°C/Gas Mark 1). Line a baking sheet with parchment (baking) paper.

For the meringue, in a large bowl, beat the egg whites until soft peaks form. Add ½ cup (4 oz/120 g) of the sugar and beat. Continue beating and adding the remaining sugar until stiff peaks form and the sugar completely dissolves.

Using a spatula, shape meringue into two 8-inch (20-cm) rounds on the baking sheet. Make a hollow in the center of one (for the bottom layer) and a peak in the center of the other (for the top layer).

Bake for 10 minutes. Reduce the heat to 225°F (110°C/Gas Mark ½) and bake for another 45–50 minutes, until meringues sound hollow when gently tapped. Remove from the oven and allow to cool on a rack.

For the chocolate hazelnut cream, fold together the cream, ground hazelnuts and half of the melted chocolate. Spread the bottom round of the meringue with the cream mixture and top with the remaining meringue round. Drizzle or pipe with the remaining chocolate and sprinkle with the hazelnuts.

Serves 8

Glossary

Here you'll find information on ingredients and techniques used in this book.

ARTICHOKES
Artichokes are the edible bud of a tall, thistle-like plant. Only the fleshy base of the leaves and the meaty bottom of the bud are eaten; the rest of the leaf and the fuzzy interior choke are discarded. Artichokes are sold fresh in various sizes; they are also available frozen, canned and marinated. Select compact, heavy globes with tightly closed leaves; refrigerate in a plastic bag for up to 4 days.

ARUGULA (ROCKET)
This green leaf vegetable has slender, multiple-lobed leaves and a peppery, slightly bitter flavor. It is used raw in salads, sandwiches and other savory dishes. Wash, then refrigerate in a plastic bag for 2–3 days.

ASPARAGUS
This tender stalk with a tightly closed bud is prized for its delicate flavor and attractive hue. Green asparagus is the most common; there are also purple and white varieties. Crisp, straight, firm stalks with a tight cap are best. Wrap in damp paper towels and refrigerate in a plastic bag for up to 4 days.

AVOCADOES
Two main varieties of tropical avocado are common: buttery Hass, with a green-black, rough skin, and blander Fuerte, with a thin, smooth skin. Ripe avocadoes yield to gentle thumb pressure. Choose firm-ripe, unblemished fruit and store in the refrigerator for several days. Ripen at warm room temperature or, more quickly, in a paper bag.

BASIL
This intensely aromatic green-leafed herb has a sweet-to-peppery licorice-like flavor that enhances tomato-based dishes and sauces, and Italian pesto. Fresh basil is plentiful in summer; dried basil, although available year round, has quite a different taste from the fresh herb. Immerse freshly cut stems in 2 inches (5 cm) of water, cover with a plastic bag and refrigerate for several days.

BAY LEAF
The pungent, woodsy leaves of the evergreen bay tree add a distinctive flavor to soups, stews and marinades, and are an essential part of a *bouquet garni*. Add whole leaves during cooking, then remove before serving. Store dried bay leaves in an airtight container in a cool, dark spot and use within a year.

BELL PEPPERS (CAPSICUMS)
Bell peppers are mildly flavored, with a crisp, crunchy texture. Green ones, which are unripe, are most common, but red, orange, yellow and purple bell peppers are also available. Bell peppers are an excellent source of vitamin C. Some red varieties are dried and ground to make paprika. Choose firm, shiny, unbruised bell peppers; avoid any with wet stems. Store for up to 5 days in the refrigerator.

CAPERS
The pickled flower buds of a Mediterranean bush, capers add a piquant note to foods. They are available salted, or in jars in brine. Store opened jars in the refrigerator. Before using, rinse off salt or drain of brine.

CHIVES
When chopped into pieces, the long, hollow green leaves of this herb add bright color and a mild onion flavor to many dishes. Fresh chives should not be wilted or damaged. Refrigerate, wrapped in damp paper towels and then in a plastic bag, for 3–4 days.

FISH SAUCE

This pungent sauce made of salted, fermented fish is used throughout Southeast Asia as a seasoning and condiment. It is available at Asian stores. If stored in a cool, dark place, it will keep indefinitely.

FRENCH, TO

A process of cutting meat and connective tissue away from the end of a rib or chop so that a portion of the bone is exposed, giving the finished product a neater look.

GARLIC

A bulb with a papery outer skin, a head of garlic consists of numerous small cloves. Although aromatic and bitter when raw, garlic becomes delicate and sweet when cooked. Fresh garlic should be plump and firm. Store whole bulbs in a cool, dark, dry place.

GINGER

The rhizome of a semitropical plant, fresh ginger has a lively, hot flavor and peppery aroma. Select firm, heavy, unshriveled stems with taut, glossy skin. Wrap in a paper towel and refrigerate for up to 2 days, or wrap airtight and freeze for longer storage.

HOT BEAN PASTE OR SAUCE

Made from a fermented soybean sauce and crushed hot chilies, this condiment thickens and enlivens all kinds of foods. Available in jars or cans in Asian markets, it stays fresh indefinitely in the refrigerator.

OLIVES AND OLIVE OIL

The fruit of the silvery-leafed olive tree, olives are either cured for eating or pressed for their oil. There are dozens of varieties, both green and black. The former are underripe, with a salty, tart flavor; they are packed pitted or unpitted in jars or cans. Pitted green olives are sometimes stuffed with red pimiento, tiny onions or whole blanched almonds. Black olives, such as Kalamatas and Niçoises, are ripe, with a smooth, mellow flavor. Only ripe olives are used for oil. For cold dishes and salad dressings, use extra-virgin oils, from the first pressing. Further pressings yield oil of lesser quality. For sauces and frying, use milder oils (labeled virgin or pure) that can better withstand being heated. Store in a dark spot away from heat for up to 6 months, or in the refrigerator for up to a year.

ONIONS
Onions can be white, yellow or reddish-purple. Green (spring) onions are immature, with more green stalk than white bulb. Store bulb onions in a cool, dark, dry place for up to 2 weeks. Refrigerate green onions in a plastic bag and use within 3–4 days.

OREGANO
Robustly flavored oregano is a favorite herb of Mediterranean cooks. Select bright green fresh oregano with firm stems; refrigerate in a plastic bag for up to 3 days. Store dried oregano in a cool, dark place.

MUSHROOMS
There are numerous varieties of edible fungi. Select firm, fresh, plump mushrooms that aren't bruised or slimy. Store in the refrigerator in paper towels or a paper bag, never in plastic. Use within 1–2 days.

PANCETTA
Unlike regular bacon, mild, spicy-sweet Italian pancetta is rarely smoked, although it is usually seasoned with pepper. It is sold in delicatessens in a roll rather than in a flat slab. Refrigerate it, well wrapped in paper then in a plastic bag, for several weeks.

PARSLEY
Curly-leaf parsley is mild, while flat-leaf (Italian) parsley is more pungent. Select healthy, lively looking bunches. Rinse and shake dry, wrap in paper towels and a plastic bag and refrigerate for up to 1 week.

PROSCIUTTO

A spicy, air-dried Italian ham, either eaten raw in thin slices or cooked as part of a recipe. Top-quality prosciutto di Parma is imported from Italy, but excellent domestic varieties are available. Italian delis and some gourmet food shops will stock both types. Wrap and refrigerate it for several weeks.

SAGE

Gray-green sage is a perennial herb, native to southern Europe, that has a slightly bitter flavor and distinctive aroma. It is widely used with poultry and in sausages. Wash the leaves and shake off excess water; wrap in paper towels and refrigerate in a plastic bag for up to 1 week. Bottled dry leaves will keep for up to 2 years and ground sage for up to 6 months.

SESAME SEEDS AND OIL

Sesame seeds add a distinctive flavor to foods and are often used as a garnish. When pressed, they yield sesame oil. Oil made from untoasted seeds is pale, with a mild flavor; that from toasted seeds is amber-colored and has a pronounced, nutty flavor. The latter is used more as a seasoning than as a cooking oil.

SHALLOTS

This small member of the onion family is formed in the same way as garlic, with a head made up of more than one clove. Shallots have a milder flavor than most onions and need only quick cooking. Look for firm, well-shaped heads that are not sprouting. Store in a cool, dry place for up to 1 month.

SHRIMP (PRAWNS)

Before cooking, fresh shrimp (prawns) are usually peeled and their thin, vein-like intestinal tracts removed. To peel and devein fresh shrimp, use your thumbs to split open the thin shell between the legs, then carefully peel it away. With a small, sharp knife, make a shallow slit along the back to expose the intestinal tract. Using the tip of the knife or your fingers, lift up and pull out the vein.

SOY SAUCE

This indispensable Asian seasoning in made from fermented soybean meal and wheat. Look for soy sauce labeled "naturally brewed"; synthetic versions made with sweeteners and artificial colors are inferior. Japanese soy sauce (*shoyu*) is less salty than Chinese types. If refrigerated, soy sauce will last indefinitely.

SQUASH/ZUCCHINI (COURGETTES)

Soft-skinned, green and yellow zucchini (courgettes), straight and crookneck squashes, and pattypan squashes are classified as "summer" vegetables, although many are sold year round. They may be used interchangeably. Choose heavy, well-shaped squash without cracks or bruises. Refrigerate for up to 4 days.

TOMATOES

Botanically a fruit, tomatoes are eaten as a vegetable. Oval-shaped plum tomatoes (also called Italian or Roma) have less juice and smaller seeds than other varieties. Tomatoes are sold fresh, or in tins sometimes flavored with basil and other seasonings. Other tinned or bottled forms include tomato paste, a highly concentrated purée; and sweet, chewy dried tomatoes, either plain or oil-packed.

THYME

Spicy and pungent, thyme is rarely used alone. More often, it is blended with other herbs to give complexity to poultry, veal and other dishes. It is sold fresh and dried. Store fresh thyme wrapped in paper towels in a plastic bag; refrigerate for 1 week. Store dried thyme for up to 2 years.

VINEGAR

Expose alcohol to a particular strain of airborne bacteria and it becomes vinegar. This acidic liquid enlivens salad dressings, marinades and sauces, as well as vegetables and noodles. There are many varieties, from fine, mellow salad vinegars, such as balsamic vinegar, to coarser types used for pickling. Vinegar lasts indefinitely, but it is best to store it away from light and heat.

Index

Entries in *italics* indicate illustrations and photos.

Acknowledgments

Photography Mark Burgin, Joe Filshie, Rowan Fotheringham, Andrew Furlong, Mike Hallson, Peter Johnson, Allen V. Lott, Ashley Mackevicius, Valerie Martin, Len Mastri, Penina, Joyce Oudkerk Pool, Allan Rosenberg, John Sims

Styling Janice Baker, Marie-Hélène Clauzon, Carolyn Fienberg, Heidi Gintner, Stephanie Greenleigh, Consuelo Guinness, Jane Hann, Melissa McClelland, Sally Parker, Jacki Passmore, Pouké, Suzie Smith, Romano Vada